THE OAKWOOD PRESS

Signal of the London & South Western Railway

A Study of Architectural Style

by G.A. Pryer

THE OAKWOOD PRESS

British Library Cataloguing in Publication Data
A Record for this book is available from the British Library
ISBN 0 85361 565 9

Typeset by Oakwood Graphics.
Repro by Ford Graphics, Ringwood, Hants.
Printed by Inkon Printers Ltd, Yateley, Hants.

Plate 2: Locomotive No. 273A engages in some shunting in the West Yard at Wimbledon *c.* 1925. The type '2' signal box was Wimbledon West, which was replaced by a new box on a different site on 28th April, 1929. This view was obviously taken from the footbridge which still spans the line at this point, but most of the sidings in the yard were removed in 1982. *Author's Collection*

Plate 1: (Title page) The type '2A' box at Ash Vale , which was provided in 1879 to control the junction with the new single line connection between Aldershot and the Ascot line. It remains in use at the time of writing, the only survivor of its type, although the lever frame has been replaced with a miniature panel. *John Scrace*

Front cover: The type '1' signal box at Broad Clyst on the Salisbury-Exeter line on 12th September, 1964. This box sustained minor damage after having been set alight by cinders from a passing train. *C.L. Caddy Collection*

Rear cover, top: An extract of the plan of Newton Tony signal box (*see Plate 126*).

Rear cover, bottom: A 'West Country' class 4-6-2 No. 34020 *Seaton* is seen passing Lymington Junction box with a Waterloo-Weymouth train on 14th October, 1960. The Lymington branch curves away to the right foreground. The signal box has definite type '3' features, but it was opened as comparatively recently as 1915 when it replaced the original structure. Why the company reverted to such an old design at this location is a mystery, the superior type '4s' having been in vogue for some 20 years by that time. It originally contained a 24-lever Stevens'-pattern frame, to which two more levers were subsequently added. On 17th October, 1978 a panel was opened in the former 'A' box at Brockenhurst, and Lymington Junction box was abolished. *Les Elsey*

Published by The Oakwood Press (Usk), P.O. Box 13, Usk, Mon., NP15 1YS.
E-mail: oakwood-press@dial.pipex.com
Website: www.oakwood-press.dial.pipex.com

Contents

Plate 3: Most type '1' boxes were of modest proportions, but there were larger examples. Andover Junction East box contained a frame of 50 levers, making it a very large installation for the 1870s. Although the ornamental valences vanished many years ago, the brick chimney stack managed to survive until gas heaters were provided around 1968. This notalgic view shows Bulleid 'Merchant Navy' class Pacific No. 35003 *Royal Mail Line* approaching the box on a down West-of-England express on 14th May, 1955. The Romsey line curved away to the right immediately behind the first coach of the train. The signal box was closed on 2nd December, 1973 when the Andover area was placed under the control of Basingstoke Panel. *R.C. Riley*

Foreword

Railways were expanding quickly during the second half of the 19th century, and needed to bolster public confidence both in their desirability as an investment and a safe and efficient mode of transport. Flimsy and poorly-appointed stations suggested that the finances and operating methods of the owning company were of a like nature, so there was a tendency to employ established architects to design suitable impressive buildings. Sir William Tite, Augustus Pugin, William Tress, and Sancton Wood, together with several other well-known architects of the Victorian era, gained much work from the railways and explored the full range of 'approved' styles from Gothic Revival to Classical. In those days architecture was bound up with morality and religion, and had important things to say about both the designer of the building and his customer. Some of the stations were ornate at the expense of practicality, and not everyone was impressed. The art critic Ruskin poured scorn on them in his *Seven Lamps of Architecture*: 'Better bury gold in the embankments than put it in ornaments on the stations . . . You would not put rings upon the fingers of a smith at his anvil'.

Ruskin's point was that railway companies should have striven towards functional designs instead of copying styles from the past , perhaps achieving a totally new but respectable 'Railway' type of architecture, but his strictures fell mostly upon deaf ears.

In the signal box we have what was perhaps the first 'true' railway building. A station might look like a country vicarage and its adjacent goods shed like a tithe barn, but seldom, and never on the London & South Western Railway (LSWR), was there any attempt to blend the signal box into the general style of the other structures, and it looked like exactly what it was.

There are several reasons for this. By the time signal boxes became widespread the public were familiar with railways and there was no need for confidence-boosting. Furthermore, they were private buildings, so ostentation was considered pointless. They also had to embrace practical considerations, such as affording the signalman a good view of the tracks and signals under his control and providing enough room beneath him to house the mechanical interlocking. There had never before been the need for such a building, except possibly the relay stations erected in the previous century in connection with the Admiralty semaphore telegraph. It is also fairly certain that no professional architect got anywhere near them.

Indeed, it is not clear who did design signal boxes, as surviving drawings are either unsigned or signed illegibly. What is certain is that on the LSWR the task devolved upon the Chief Civil Engineer's staff, perhaps because they were thought best qualified to assess the suitability of sites for different types of building. Some were undoubtedly 'off the peg' structures straight out a contractor's catalogue, but most of the early boxes appear to have been designed from within the railway company, as were all those after 1878 except for a few ground-level boxes.

This work attempts to outline the development in signal box design from the earliest years to the end of the LSWR as an independent company. It does not set out to be a history of railway signalling as such, although of course some mention of it is unavoidable. The task has been a complex one, for unlike its

Southern neighbours the London, Brighton & South Coast Railway (LBSCR) and South Eastern & Chatham Railway (SECR), or even the GWR with whom it shared so much territory, the 'South Western' never adhered rigidly to sets of standard drawings, and produced a lot of variants of so-called 'standard' structures. They also put up completely non-standard boxes for no apparent reason, and sometimes harked back to an obsolete design when installing new signalling, making it impossible to 'date' anything according to its style of architecture. Several brave attempts to categorise these boxes have been made before, notably by members of both the Signalling Record Society and the South Western Circle, but the author has always felt that more sub-divisions in the categories were required in order to do justice to the subject. The trouble is that the deeper the researcher digs the more cavernous becomes the hole into which he is liable to fall. For example, in *The Signal Box* (Oxford Publishing Co., 1986) the Signalling Study Group (alias various members of the Signalling Record Society) made a serious and praiseworthy attempt at categorising LSWR signal boxes, yet managed to fall into the trap of allocating a separate class, '3C', to those on the North Cornwall Line. It was an easy mistake to make, as those boxes certainly did appear somewhat different to the general run of standard designs, and the Study Group was writing about the whole of Britain and could not therefore get over-involved with a single company, but closer scrutiny has revealed them to be basically type '3' structures which had gone through a degree of evolution because of the length of time taken to construct the line and, probably, because local contractors were employed.

Another problem is that many boxes underwent considerable alterations during their lifetimes, and some detective work is necessary in order to decide how they looked originally and therefore to which class they belonged. The various type '3s' are the worst in this respect. A few, apparently, had ornamental valences whilst others did not, and the small box-type roof ventilator which seemed to be a standard component of these boxes was sometimes removed in later years to give them an entirely different outline. Indeed, some of the later structures in this class seem never to have had them, being fitted with 'torpedo' vents instead. Because of all these difficulties the text has had to be supplemented by extended captions to the photographs, which it is hoped will make the various types more readily understandable.

There will certainly be those who disagree with some of the author's findings, but if it keeps the debate alive and encourages more in-depth research the book will have achieved something. Whilst there are still a few pockets of mechanical signalling around the country, the signal box is becoming quite a rare building and will probably vanish altogether over the next 20 years. It was not just the workplace of generations of dedicated railwaymen but also a way of life, and it should not be allowed to disappear before the march of 'progress' without adequate record.

George Pryer,
Dorchester,
Dorset.

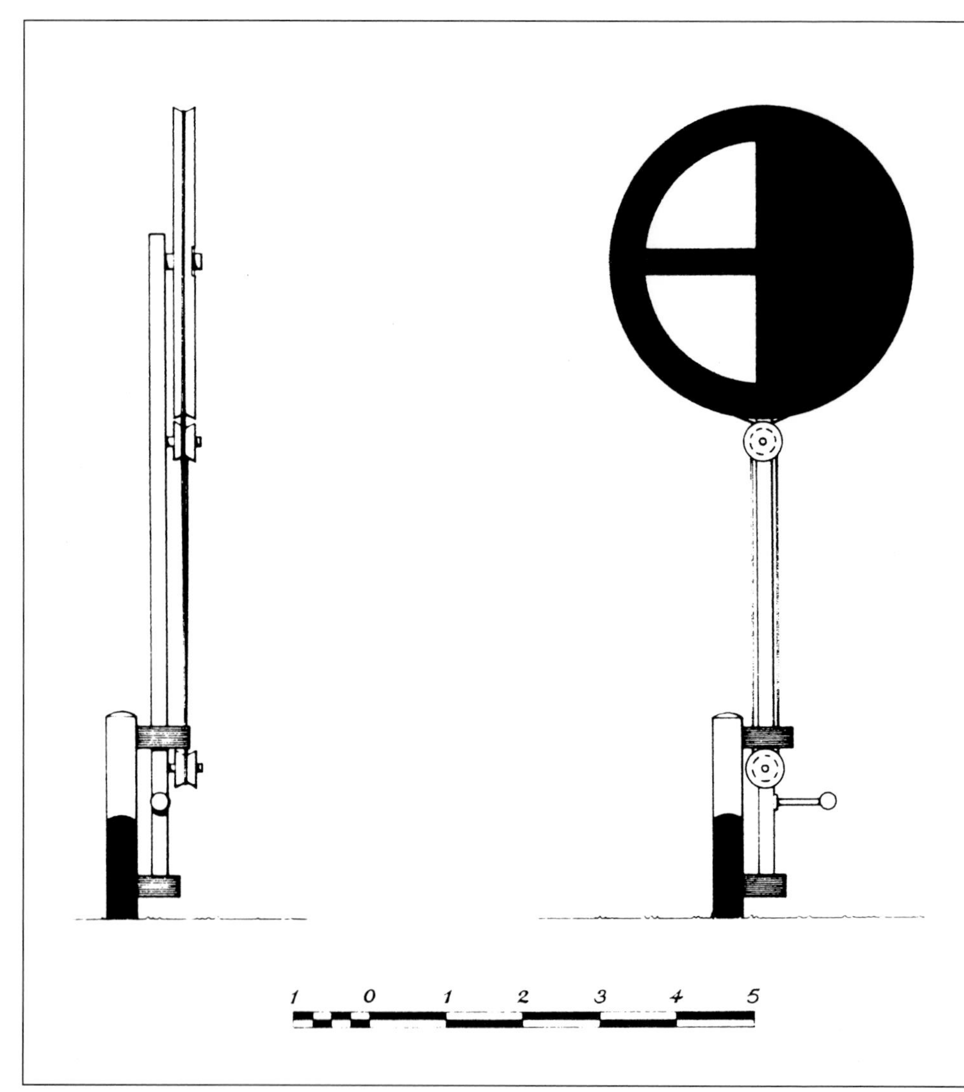

Plate 4: A revolving disc signal designed by Albinus Martin, as used on the LSWR from the earliest times until the introduction of proper lever frames. The left-hand drawing shows the signal in the 'both lines clear' position, with the disc turned parallel to the track and virtually invisible to approaching trains. That on the right shows it indicating 'left-hand line only clear, right-hand line blocked'. When the disc was rotated to display both apertures at the bottom both lines were blocked. At night oil lamps gave the appropriate indications. The discs were revolved by rope and pulley, whilst the mast was turned by a handle to give the 'end-on' view. Because of the variety of movements required in the operation of these signals they were unsuitable for operation from conventional levers.

Chapter One

The Early Years

The earliest railways had no signalling system whatsoever, but by the time this new mode of transport reached the South of England this had ceased to be entirely true. Primitive hand-worked signals, on the LSWR taking the form of large revolving discs under the control of 'Policemen', were erected at a point somewhere near the station office and in such a position that they could be easily seen by the drivers of approaching trains. They were designed to apply to traffic in both directions, and gave authority for movements to enter the station, but there were no starting signals and permission to proceed to the next place was given verbally or by hand signal. Some of these disc signals were of great height to improve their visibility, although this must have been somewhat counter-productive in foggy weather. Furthermore, they did not tell drivers where to stop, this being left to their better judgement. Of course, there was no interlocking between these signals and any points in the route, so trains occasionally became 'wrong-roaded' because somebody had altered the points without consulting the policeman. Safe working was achieved mainly through the low speeds at which trains approached such signals, giving the drivers time to stop if they noticed something wrong even with the inadequate braking then available.

Signal boxes did not exist. At isolated junctions a hut (sometimes dignified with the term 'observatory') would be provided for the policeman, but at stations these officers had other duties to perform such as attending to the security of goods and parcels, keeping order when large crowds descended for excursion trains, and ejecting trespassers. He therefore shared the main office with the station clerk, and signalled trains as required between his other jobs. The levers he operated were attached to the signal posts or on the ground beside the points, and were therefore scattered all over the layout. Information about train running was received and sent by the electric telegraph, which was operated by the clerk rather than the policeman who gained such details secondhand. Furthermore, the telegraph was not used solely for traffic purposes, and would often be busy with other business.

Seen in the light of modern safety practices, the whole system of train working in those far-off days seems extremely hazardous. Yet there were very few serious accidents, and the railway was considerably safer than any other form of transport available at the time. A few people were killed or injured, and for some reason such events caused public concern much greater than that expressed when a stage coach overturned or a sailing ship foundered on a rocky shore, concern which led to a 'Regulation of Railways Act' in 1840. Unlike subsequent Acts, it gave the Government no influence over operating matters and was more concerned with avoiding monopolies in the field of rail transport, but it did send a warning shot across the bows of the early companies to the effect that their activities were being watched, even though they remained free (at least for the time being) to adopt such rules, regulations and equipment as they saw fit. The Railway Department of the Board of Trade was formed under this Act, and it was this body that would in the future insist on set standards of signalling. Another Act two years later empowered the Board of Trade to conduct rigorous inspections of all new lines before they could be opened for traffic, but these were mainly concerned with the quality of the engineering works. An inspector could refuse permission for a line to open if the bridges were weak, but he could only make recommendations if the method of working failed to impress him, recommendations which the owning company was at liberty to ignore, and often did!

In order to understand the manner in which the railways were operated in the mid-19th century we have to discard all our current notions about how things are done and remember that the world was then a very different place. With only the horse and cart for competition and a virtual monopoly of inland transport, it is tempting to think that railways were very busy, but in fact that was not the case. Only the wealthy travelled, and then not on a regular basis except for a few country MPs travelling between Parliament and their constituencies. Villages and towns were self-sufficient, and the poor, who had never been in a position to travel, saw no reason to start doing so even if they could have afforded the fares. The reality was that four or five trains each way per day catered adequately for most flows of traffic, anything in excess of that being reckoned a really good service. Speeds were very moderate, but must have seemed spectacular enough at more than twice the speed of a galloping horse! With traffic at that sort of level it required a combination of unspeakable folly and downright bad luck to create any sort of accident (except possibly derailment), and a sophisticated signalling system was about the last thing upon which railway managers wanted to expend money.

However, by about 1855 trains were increasing in both speed and frequency as people adopted the travel habit and new industries flourished where they had previously been hampered by lack of transport, and the somewhat free-and-easy methods of working were causing concern. There were reports of whole train-loads of passengers descending onto station platforms during the lengthy stops then common, and standing there until the guard blew his whistle for departure, rather than remain seated in the carriages and risk being run into by a following train! The telegraph (already mentioned) was some help in keeping trains spaced out, but the rather relaxed way in which it was used was unsatisfactory. For instance, trains were wired forward but not 'Blocked Back', in other words, there was no 'Train out of Section' message. It was customary for the clerk to advise the next station of the imminent dispatch of a train, but as the man at the other end was usually busy with other matters he did not necessarily await a reply but simply sent it once the prescribed interval of time since the last train had elapsed. Furthermore, there developed the rather reprehensible habit of the telegraph instrument being operated by whoever happened to be about at the time. The policeman could, unbeknown to the clerk, wander down the line in search of an overdue train, but in his absence the clerk could acknowledge a message and give the impression that all was well.

At large and busy stations there was the additional complication of 'Pointsmen', who ran around setting points at the direction of the policeman.

The latter was supposed to await confirmation that all the relevant points had been set before turning the signal to 'clear', but there must have been many trains diverted to the wrong lines through a pointsman missing a set or assuming that either the policeman or another pointsman was going to attend to that part of the layout. In short, the electric telegraph provided a chain of communication along the line, but it was not wholly dependable as a signalling system and the signals themselves were still free to conflict with the points.

A description of the early LSWR signal has already been given, but the familiar semaphore was also to be found in some places, having been standard on a few railways, albeit in a crude form, since 1841. Some of the original semaphores had three positions, horizontal for 'Stop', lowered to 45 degrees for 'Caution', and invisible to drivers by dropping vertically into a slot within the post for 'All Clear'. It need hardly be said that an invisible signal as a clear indication was far from satisfactory, as should the arm become broken or jammed in its slot the impression would be given that the line was clear even if the previous train had only just left! It was the very opposite of later signalling practice which required everything to 'fail safe'.

By the 1850s it must have been obvious to the railway authorities that, at least at the busier stations, a safer and more efficient method of working was required, and that the best way of achieving this would be to concentrate all the levers in one place. However, it was also seen that until some form of interlocking was devised, lever concentration could actually increase the dangers. At least with the existing arrangement the policeman or one of his assistants had to walk the route to set it up, whereas concentrated levers free of locking would enable him to stand in one place and clear the signals regardless of the route set. Despite this concern, the Board of Trade insisted on lever concentration for all new works after 1858, doubtless in the hope that a guaranteed market for their work would spur inventors into designing suitable equipment. Existing layouts were allowed to carry on as before.

Enterprising individuals and engineering companies were not slow to see the business potential of railway signalling. Stevens and Son, of Southwark Bridge Road, London, had started trading as gas and general engineers in 1820, becoming involved with railways in 1830 when they were contracted to build some revolving signals for the London and Southampton line. In 1839 they were advertising a 'junction platform' consisting of levers mounted upon a wooden stage with a small hut for the operator, but apparently the Board of Trade did not approve of it. Their first interlocked frame was produced in 1860.

Also in 1860 an employee of the LBSCR, John Saxby, built a lever frame with crude interlocking for use at London's Victoria station, and three years later he went into partnership with John Stinson Farmer to form the well-known signalling contracting business of Saxby and Farmer. Interlocking at that time was very basic, and suitable only for small and simple layouts, but it was better than nothing, and its availability made the concentration of levers at busy stations a realistic proposition.

There is no doubt that a few recognisable signal boxes appeared at key locations on the LSWR at about that time, although the method of working remained a combination of timetable and telegraph rather than any kind of Block

Typical Wayside Station (1868)

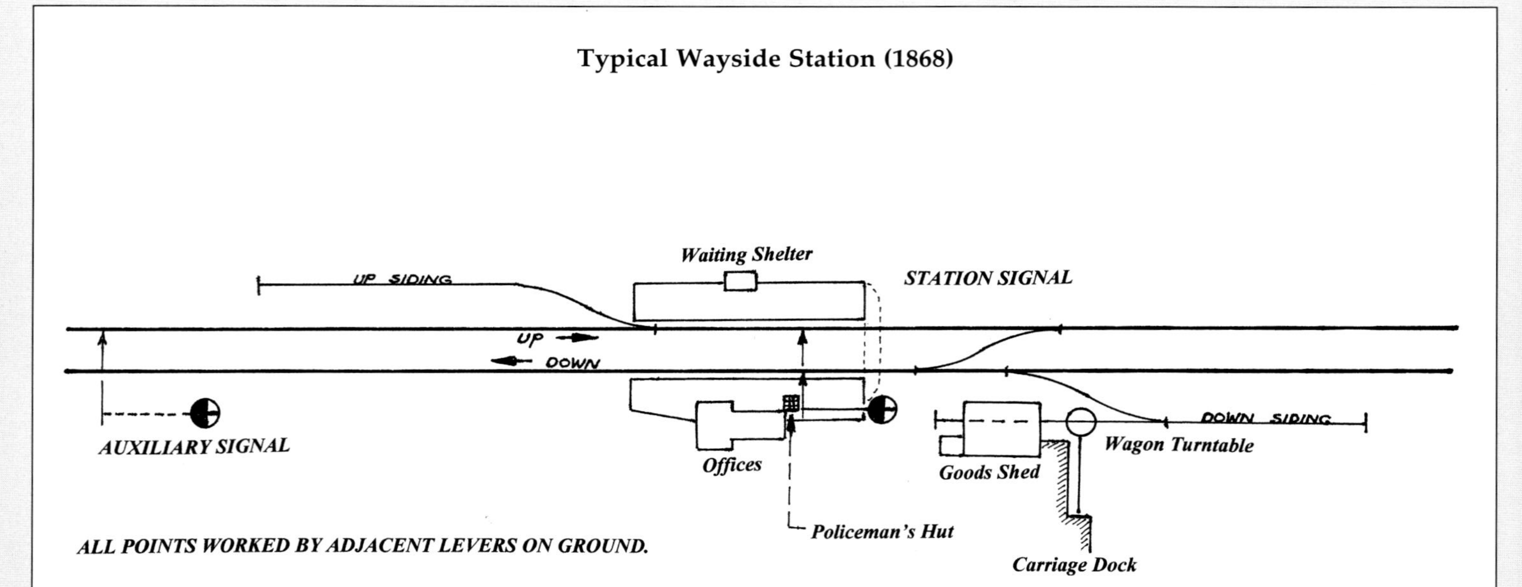

Plate 5: This diagram illustrates the basic arrangements to be found at a typical small station in the days before interlocking. Note that only one 'stop' signal is provided (in the illustration showing both lines 'Blocked'). Auxiliaries, which were the forerunners of the 'Distant' signals, were not always provided if the approach view of the station signal was deemed to be adequate. Drivers of trains approaching a signal as shown would be expected to bring their trains to a stand before passing over any of the pointwork. A handsignal or verbal instruction would be given by the policeman to proceed towards the next station.

System. These early lever frames were small, as only a few signals were provided and it had not yet become obligatory to fit facing point locks, and their use was confined to a few busy junctions or stations which carried out a great amount of shunting. Where lever frames were installed semaphore arms replaced the old discs, but elsewhere the policeman continued with his duties as before.

The Block System had been devised in 1853 and a few progressive lines made immediate use of it, but generally the companies were reluctant on grounds of cost, some even arguing against it on the somewhat spurious grounds that 'gadgets' tended to remove the need for personal vigilance by the operating staff, and were therefore dangerous. The public were suspicious that railway Directors had a greater interest in the pockets of their shareholders than in the safety of their customers, but it must be borne in mind that the Block System was only of any real value when an entire line was fitted with it, and the level of traffic on many routes was still sufficiently low that it could be seen as an expensive luxury.

William Henry Preece joined the Electric Telegraph Company in 1853, becoming familiar with railways the following year when that company was contracted to install an early form of Block Working on the London & North Western Railway. The subject fascinated him to the extent that he devoted much of his limited spare time to designing better equipment, and in 1860 he joined the LSWR as telegraph superintendent. Just two years later he designed some instruments of his own, his position with the company allowing him make a trial installation between the GWR signal box at Exeter St David's and Exeter Queen Street. The choice of that section, remote as it was from the seat of LSWR power, is hard to explain, but possibly the steep gradient and tunnel made it a difficult one to operate and therefore just the sort of place that would benefit from Block Working. The section was also short, so the initial installation costs would have been fairly low.

As the basis of his instruments Preece adopted miniature semaphore arms, almost exact replicas of the 'outdoor' signals controlling the trains, one arm being provided for each direction of travel. The indications were very simple and mirrored those of the 'outdoor' signals. When the arm was lowered the signalman was free to clear the relevant signals and admit a train to the section ahead, but when it was horizontal the trains had to be stopped. At the time small semaphore arms were better than dials or pointers, as the interiors of early signal boxes were very dark and gloomy - particularly at night - and arms were easier to see. The system required only one line wire, making it relatively cheap to install. True 'open block' was practised, the line being considered normally clear unless actually occupied by a train, a curiously modern notion found today in Track Circuit Block. This pilot installation was thoroughly successful, but the universal application of it had to await further legislation and the subsequent spread of proper signal boxes, although a few other sections were converted to Block Working in the meantime.

A few signal boxes appeared between 1862 and 1871, but their use was confined to junctions, always seen as a potential source of danger, and stations where the volume of traffic or amount of shunting made the concentration of levers beneficial. Each box was dealt with as an individual project, and there was no standard design. Some of the stranger and more exotic buildings date from this period. It is not known who designed them but they appeared as two main types, one of which employed the methods of building later seen in the Types One to Three where the ground floor was of brick or stone masonry surmounted by a largely wooden upper storey, much of which was window. Often there was some ornamental carpentry, and sometimes the roofs were covered with sheet lead or tarred canvas. However, there seems to have been a preference for all-brick structures with fairly small windows and slate roofs from which decoration was totally absent, except possibly for ornamental barge-boards.

During this period the operating advantages of interlocked frames over isolated point and signal levers became very obvious, and by 1869 there were some 1,500 'proper' signal boxes on the railways of Britain, although the number actually on the lines of the LSWR is not recorded. The Board of Trade were trying to encourage both locking and Block Working, but stopped short of insisting upon it. They did, however, make it clear that they expected to see it in connection with all new works, and another Regulation of Railways Act of 1871 extended their powers from the inspection solely of new lines to alterations at existing places. The LSWR took the hint, and from that year all new lines, junctions, and siding connections were fitted up with locking frames from the start. Frames available at the time were fairly crude, but in 1873 Stevens and Son patented an improved version with tappet locking which not only facilitated the control of more complicated layouts but enabled that company to take full advantage of another parliamentary Act, passed the same year, which obliged all railway companies to adopt certain signalling standards. These included progress towards full interlocking, the provision of facing point locks (FPLs), and the adoption of the Absolute Block System on all passenger-carrying lines. The railway companies were required to furnish the Board of Trade with regular returns on the progress made, and although one or two of the more impoverished lines were reluctant to comply, the LSWR and most of the other major companies were anxious not to appear on the Government's 'black list' and hurriedly installed the necessary equipment. This caused much feverish activity in the world of signal engineering and brought about the formation of many firms of contractors.

Although the LSWR by no means lagged behind other railways in its provision of interlocking there was much work to be done, and signal boxes needed to be quick and easy to construct from a range of 'off the peg' parts. For the first time a standard design was called for, and the type '1' box was born! By 1875 the company could claim that 68 per cent of its locations were interlocked at a time when only the London railways (Metropolitan, District, and North London) were able to furnish 100 per cent returns, a very creditable effort in view of the size of the system, but the enormity of the task can be judged from the fact that it was 1889 before it was completed. Some of the last boxes in this batch must have been scrambled together in unseemly haste, as 1889 was the year of the final Regulation of Railways Act under which interlocking and Block Working became absolutely compulsory.

The Block System had spread somewhat faster than interlocking as it was much easier to install, small huts being provided to house the instruments whilst the old hand-worked points and signals continued in use pending the erection of a proper signal box. As work progressed these huts could be moved elsewhere to allow yet further extensions to Block Working.

On many railways this sudden spread of proper signalling spelled the end of non-standard signal boxes, but this was not the case on the LSWR where, for some unknown reason, buildings of strange design continued to appear from time to time. The non-standard boxes of the company therefore fall into two distinct groups: those which pre-date the 1873 Act of Parliament for which opening dates are not always available, and later ones where the opening date is known, and which logically should have been erected to one of the standard designs and yet were individualistic. Perhaps one explanation for some of the latter can be found in the last-minute structures required under the 1889 Act. With a dead-line for compliance and possibly a shortage of standard parts, the Civil Engineer might well have been pressed into using whatever materials were to hand, including window frames and the like ordered for different types of building.

In this first chapter we will look at some of the earliest boxes installed on the LSWR of which photographs are available. There must have been many more - some of them doubtless very interesting buildings - but the railway photographer was a rare animal until the end of the 19th century, and when he did indulge in his hobby he tended to concentrate on trains or locomotives rather than signalling subjects. Most of the early boxes therefore vanished without record, but some of them lasted long enough to attract the attention of modern photographers.

Plate 6: The 11.16 am Bournemouth West to York passes Southampton Tunnel Junction box on 23rd May, 1953, hauled by 'Battle of Britain' class No. 34109 *Sir Trafford Leigh-Mallory*. This was one of the early signal boxes, similar in style to that at Milford Goods (Salisbury) - *see Plate 10*. A junction was formed at this point in 1858 with the opening of the Northam Curve, but as this predated interlocking the control of traffic must originally have been by a policeman in a small hut. Doubtless this was improved as soon as locking frames became generally available, so the structure shown here could date from around 1861. The arrangement of the 13-lever frame (later increased to 14) was unusual in being end-on to trains instead of parallel to the track! The box gave good service, lasting for more than a century. It was closed on 2nd October, 1966 when control was transferred to Northam Junction box. *Pamlin Prints*

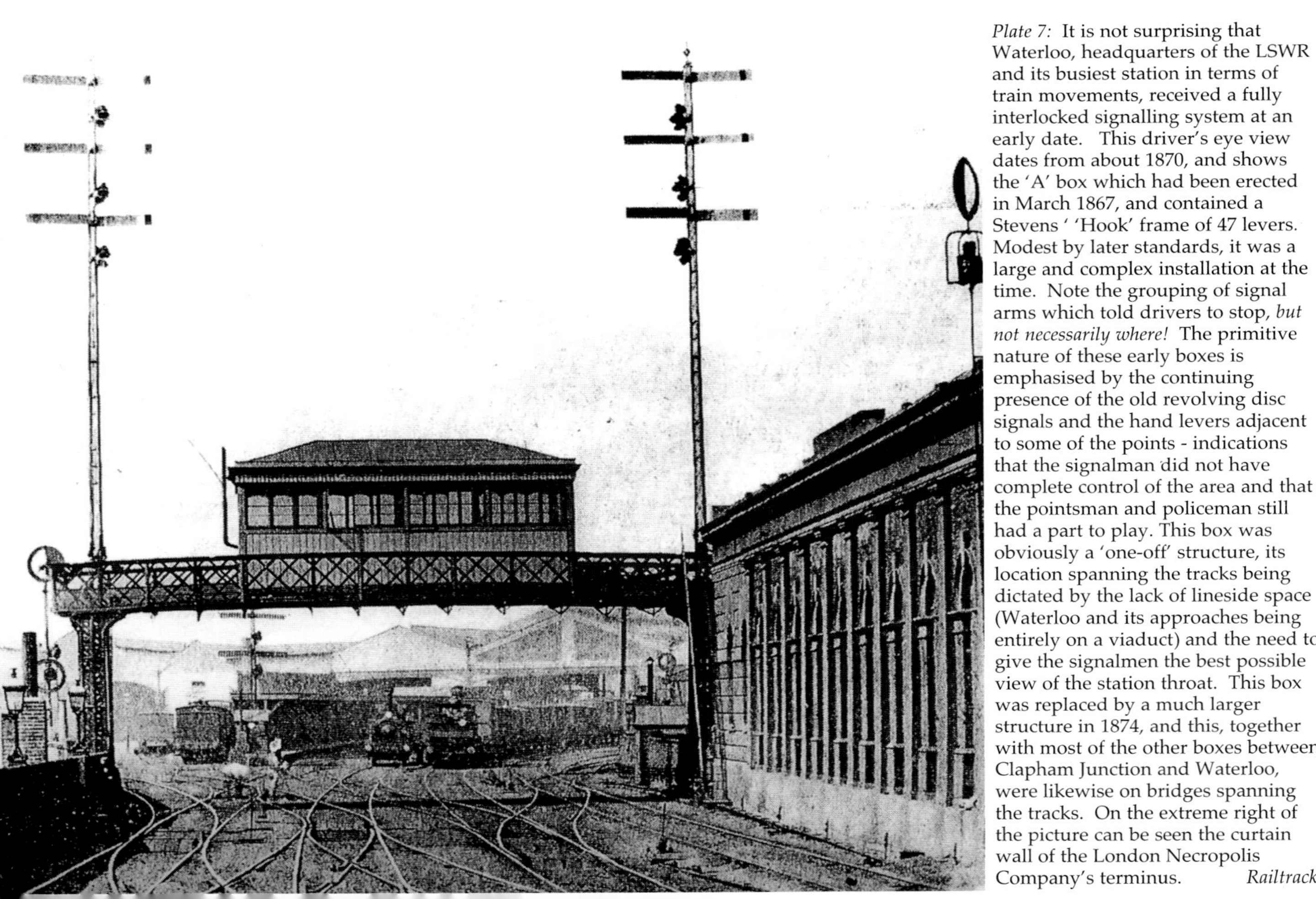

Plate 7: It is not surprising that Waterloo, headquarters of the LSWR and its busiest station in terms of train movements, received a fully interlocked signalling system at an early date. This driver's eye view dates from about 1870, and shows the 'A' box which had been erected in March 1867, and contained a Stevens ' 'Hook' frame of 47 levers. Modest by later standards, it was a large and complex installation at the time. Note the grouping of signal arms which told drivers to stop, *but not necessarily where!* The primitive nature of these early boxes is emphasised by the continuing presence of the old revolving disc signals and the hand levers adjacent to some of the points - indications that the signalman did not have complete control of the area and that the pointsman and policeman still had a part to play. This box was obviously a 'one-off' structure, its location spanning the tracks being dictated by the lack of lineside space (Waterloo and its approaches being entirely on a viaduct) and the need to give the signalmen the best possible view of the station throat. This box was replaced by a much larger structure in 1874, and this, together with most of the other boxes between Clapham Junction and Waterloo, were likewise on bridges spanning the tracks. On the extreme right of the picture can be seen the curtain wall of the London Necropolis Company's terminus. *Railtrack*

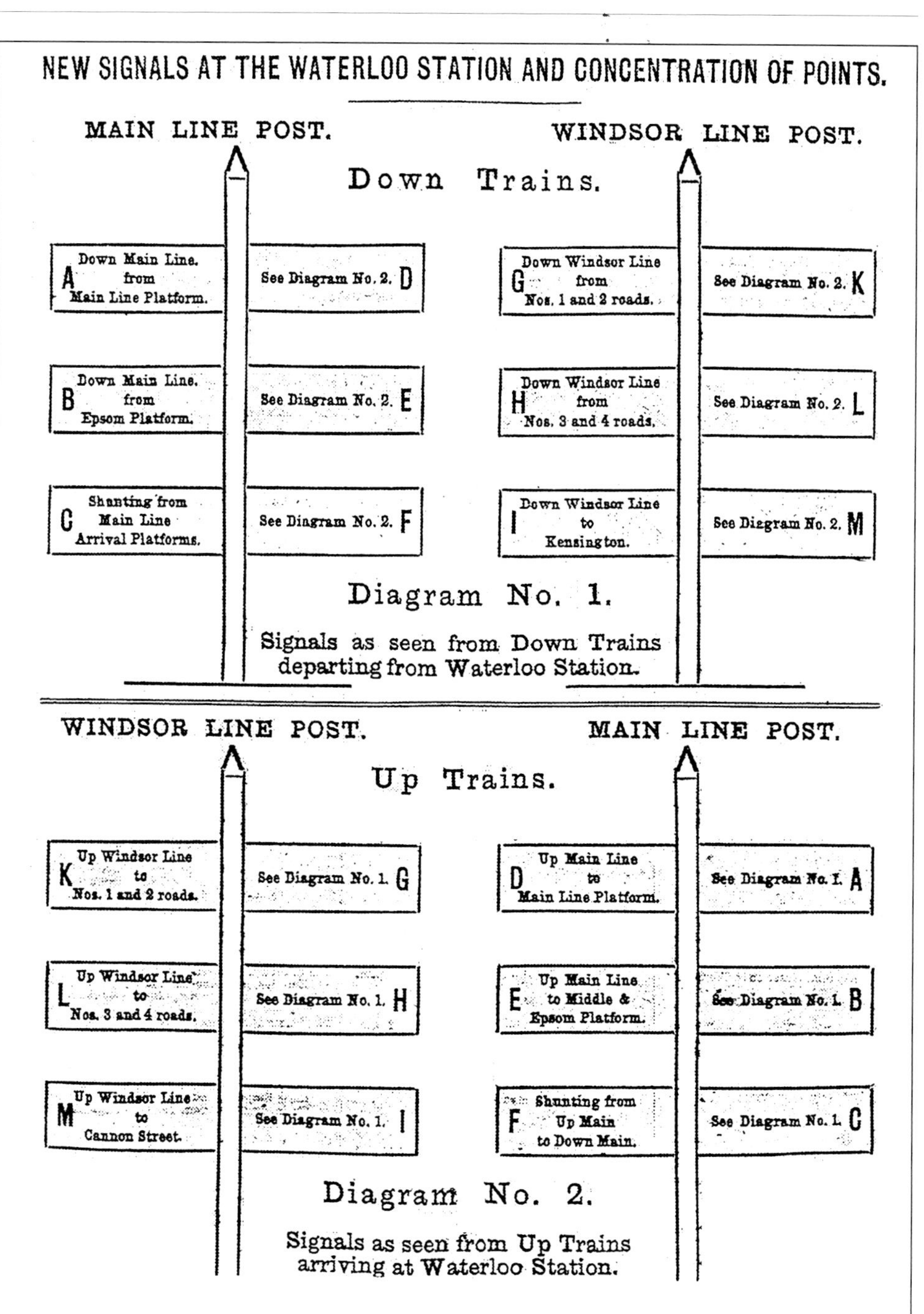
NEW SIGNALS AT THE WATERLOO STATION AND CONCENTRATION OF POINTS.

MAIN LINE POST.

WINDSOR LINE POST.

Down Trains.

Main Line Post (left arm)	Main Line Post (right arm)	Windsor Line Post (left arm)	Windsor Line Post (right arm)
A Down Main Line from Main Line Platform.	See Diagram No. 2. D	G Down Windsor Line from Nos. 1 and 2 roads.	See Diagram No. 2. K
B Down Main Line, from Epsom Platform.	See Diagram No. 2. E	H Down Windsor Line from Nos. 3 and 4 roads.	See Diagram No. 2. L
C Shunting from Main Line Arrival Platforms.	See Diagram No. 2. F	I Down Windsor Line to Kensington.	See Diagram No. 2. M

Diagram No. 1.

Signals as seen from Down Trains departing from Waterloo Station.

WINDSOR LINE POST.

MAIN LINE POST.

Up Trains.

Windsor Line Post (left arm)	Windsor Line Post (right arm)	Main Line Post (left arm)	Main Line Post (right arm)
K Up Windsor Line to Nos. 1 and 2 roads.	See Diagram No. 1. G	D Up Main Line to Main Line Platform.	See Diagram No. 1. A
L Up Windsor Line to Nos. 3 and 4 roads.	See Diagram No. 1. H	E Up Main Line to Middle & Epsom Platform.	See Diagram No. 1. B
M Up Windsor Line to Cannon Street.	See Diagram No. 1. I	F Shunting from Up Main to Down Main.	See Diagram No. 1. C

Diagram No. 2.

Signals as seen from Up Trains arriving at Waterloo Station.

Plate 8: Explanation of the signals at the throat of Waterloo station as published in the Working Time Table of April 1867. *Railtrack*

Plate 9: 'Godalming Junction' came into existence in 1859, when the opening of the Portsmouth Direct line by-passed the original terminal station. Lever concentration was already a legal requirement by that date, but as proper interlocked frames did not exist there was probably an open stage upon which stood a hut for the policeman and the few levers required to operate a basic layout. The structure shown here is identical to the Saxby 'boxes on stilts' erected on the LBSCR, and was no doubt an improvement carried out around 1863. By the time this photograph was taken in November 1892, junction signals of a fairly 'modern' appearance had replaced whatever had been there previously, probably arms mounted on a common post as in the earlier picture of Waterloo. The platelayers in the foreground seem very interested in the antics of the photographer: a man wielding a camera would have been something of a novelty to ordinary working folk at that time! In 1897 a new station was opened nearby to serve the growing suburb of Farncombe and two new type '4' boxes were provided. The functions of Godalming Junction box were then taken over by Farncombe West.

Surrey History Service

Plate 10: The opening date of this very Victorian box at Milford Goods (Salisbury) is not recorded. It contained a Stevens' frame of 28 levers (5 of which were push-and-pull) the layout of which suggested that the installation dated from the days of Milford as a passenger station. However, Milford was relegated to a goods depot in May 1859 - one year after lever concentration became obligatory for new works but just before the invention of interlocked frames - so its early history is shrouded in mystery. It is probable that the volume of shunting carried out at Milford, which remained the City's main goods yard until the rebuilding of Salisbury station in 1902, was seen to justify a locking frame at an early date, and this box might have been erected as early as 1861. It remained in use until 1st January, 1968, latterly with a lot of spare levers! Note the very ornate valences; later boxes used simpler patterns. For many years the box suffered from sunken foundations, the signalmen walking down quite a steep slope from the doorway towards the fireplace, and some evidence of this 'lean' is apparent from the photograph. A very similar box was at Southampton Tunnel Junction (*Plate 6*).

G.F. Gillham

Plate 11: Salisbury boasted another antique box - Tunnel Junction - which may be even older than Milford and dated from 1859 when the new lines through Salisbury came into use. Certainly lever concentration was obligatory in this case, as it was a 'new junction', but interlocking in the accepted sense of the term was not available. The initial installation must have been extremely basic, because in later years the provision of conventional signalling required a frame of 19 levers which filled the building to capacity. Indeed, so cramped was the interior of this box, that the signalmen's lockers and a small wash basin had to be located in the lean-to porch. This early box was in sharp contrast to its neighbour at Milford, being totally devoid of ornamentation. It was, however, typical of the 'all brick' structures erected prior to 1873. It enjoyed a remarkably long life, surviving until 17th August, 1981 when the whole area came under the control of a panel at Salisbury.

G.F. Gillham

Plate 12: The Kingston-New Malden line was opened in January 1869 and was therefore given signal boxes right from the start. Most boxes in the area had been replaced by the early years of the 20th century, Norbiton alone surviving as an example of the type of boxes provided on a newly-opened line in the days before a standard design was available. The building was virtually square in section, the wooden superstructure being mounted on the sort of plain brick tower usually associated with water tanks. There was horizontal boarding below the windows and vertical boards between the windows and the eaves. The apex roof was slated and fitted with a 'torpedo' vent, and there was a brick chimney stack for the open coal fire. This box gave just over a century of service, being abolished on 27th July, 1969. *John Scrace*

New Poole Junction (1877)

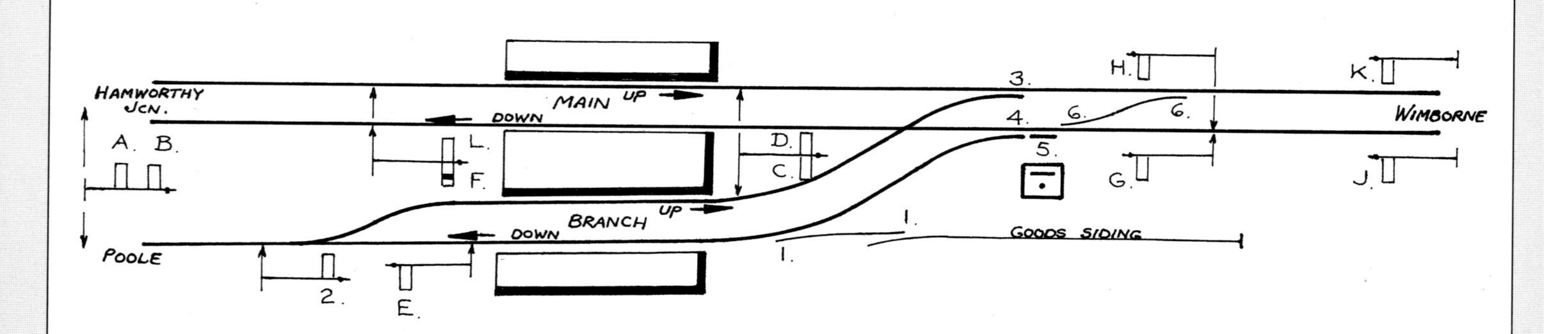

Plate 13: New Poole Junction (later 'Broadstone') was one of the pre-Block Working lever frame boxes dating from 1872. It is interesting that at that time there does not even appear to have been a definite policy towards the numbering of levers, and many of them are lettered. The diagram gives no clue as to the method of operation of the points in the single line coming from Poole, but as they would have been outside the distance allowed for mechanical working they must have been on a ground frame. Note that the down homes and 'Auxiliaries' were two separate posts - one each side of the line - instead of the later standard arrangement of a bracket signal with two dolls.

Plate 14: Broadstone box (originally 'New Poole Junction') dated from the opening of the Poole and Bournemouth Railway in December 1872, at which time it contained a frame of 17 levers. It was doubled in size in 1886 when the Somerset & Dorset's new Corfe Mullen cut-off also made a junction at this point, the newer brickwork of the extension at the right-hand end of the building being evident in this photograph. In connection with this work a Stevens' frame of 33 levers was installed. At some stage additional windows were inserted in the ground floor, giving the front elevation a somewhat cluttered appearance, but otherwise it provides a good example of the early 'all brick' design, although the provision of a railed walkway in front of the windows was unusual in this type of box. Around 1950 this box received a Westinghouse 'A2' frame of 32 levers, secondhand from Lockerley (between Dean and Dunbridge), and this was fitted - SR fashion - along the back wall of the box, although it made no difference to its external appearance. Broadstone box remained open until 18th October, 1970.

C.L. Caddy

Plate 15: As with so many early boxes, the opening date of this box at Winchester ('Winchester City' after September 1949) is not recorded, but it followed the trend of providing interlocking at key stations ahead of the main programme and was probably installed in the mid-1860s. It was typical of its type, being devoid of all decoration, and the operating floor was elevated to only about 5 feet instead of the later standard of 8 feet. Of the front windows only the two end frames were sliding, the central one being fixed. The lever frame contained 21 levers. This box was closed on 1st November, 1960, when it was replaced by a modern mechanical box of BR design.
B.L. Jackson Collection

Plate 16: Although no documentary evidence has come to light, this lofty brick box at Wimborne would seem to date from 1860 when the opening of the first section of the Dorset Central made this an important junction with considerable shunting. Its importance was enhanced further in 1866 with the opening of the line between West Moors and Salisbury, and although Block Working was not extended over the Southampton & Dorchester line in general until the 1870s, Wimborne, then classed as the busiest junction in Dorset, must have been an early candidate for interlocking. This box, which contained a Stevens' frame of 23 levers (extended to 29 in 1933), was unusually tall because the whole layout was on a curve and the view from a box of normal height would have been greatly impeded by the station buildings and platform canopies. The window arrangement, with those lighting the locking room balancing those of the operating floor, was unique. All-brick boxes of this height were also extremely rare, the company preferring to use timber when extreme elevation was necessary. Wimborne box was converted to a ground frame (surely the tallest on record) in July 1966 following the withdrawal of passenger services in the area, being finally abolished on 8th January, 1967. *G.F. Gillham*

Plate 17: Farnham Junction was one of the comparatively few early boxes that can be positively dated, it being opened in 1870 in connection with the new lines through Aldershot. Although all-brick structures were then in vogue, the use of timber in this instance was dictated by the instability of the site. Because of an adjacent road bridge, it was necessary to build this box halfway up the side of the cutting in order to elevate the signalman to a position where he could see approaching trains, and a weighty brick box would have created difficulties. The slightly overhanging top was most unusual, but the grouping of the windows at the two front corners later appeared as a standard feature of LSWR design in the type '4' boxes, although it was rare enough at the time. The box survived virtually unaltered until abolition on 5th May, 1964, even the saw-tooth valence and chimney-style metal roof vent remaining intact. Latterly it had been seldom opened, the junction having been taken out in November 1954. *M. Lawson*

Plate 18: Not all signal boxes were built as such, this one at Totton being a conversion from a Southampton & Dorchester Railway crossing keeper's cottage. The little brick pediment over what was once the front door of the residence can be discerned behind the wooden fencing. The date of the conversion is not known, but is thought to have been around 1870. Because the operating floor was built on top of what was originally a bungalow dwelling, the box was exceptionally spacious for one of its period, which was just as well as things turned out, for several extensions to the layout were made over the years. Originally called 'Eling Crossing', this box originally contained just 17 levers. This was increased to 22 in 1895, and again to 35 in 1925 when the opening of the branch to Fawley caused it to be renamed 'Eling Junction'. In February 1950 it became 'Totton' to match the name of the adjacent station. Over all these years the external appearance of the box changed very little, although the slate roof gave way to corrugated asbestos in BR days, which ruined the look of the building. By the time this photograph was taken, some of the window frames had been renewed. Totton box lasted until 28th February, 1982, when the area was taken over by Eastleigh panel box.

B.L. Jackson

Plate 19: The Petersfield side of Buriton box, showing the external stairs and porch.
John Scrace

Plate 20 The 'country' side of the box. The very small window in the end wall would seem to be an addition, but otherwise the building underwent few changes throughout its existence.
John Scrace

The opening date of this unusual box at Buriton Siding (near Petersfield) is unrecorded, and is indeed something of a mystery since the Board of Trade report on the doubling of the Petersfield-Rowlands Castle section in 1878 makes no mention of it, yet another report of 1883 describes the box as 'old'. It had about it the air of a 'Police Station', a point where policemen were stationed to regulate traffic in the days before Block Working - and it was exactly the kind of location where such a post would have been established, the section involving heavy gradients and a tunnel, all on reverse curves. Almost certainly it was not built for its later purpose, as the original lever frame held only 7 levers for which the structure was much too large. In around 1900 the number of levers was doubled, but there was still quite a lot of room in the box! Brick signal boxes with gable roofs were never very common, but it was even rarer to have the gable end towards the track. The box survived until 11th January, 1970.

Plate 21: The extension of the line from Bideford to Torrington was opened on 18th July, 1872, and would have therefore come under the provisions of the 1871 Act of Parliament, obliging the company to install interlocking from the outset. This photograph of Torrington is evidence that no standard designs for boxes were available prior to the type '1' of 1873, for it is built in a very individualistic style. Right up to window sill level rubble masonry was used, above which were very distinctive four-pane windows whose uprights extended up to the eaves. Horizontal boards, applied internally, filled the spaces between these uprights. The two sets of window frames at each end were sliding but the two in the middle were fixed. This box was considerably altered by the Southern Railway, probably in 1925 when the North Devon & Cornwall Junction Light Railway made an end-on junction at Torrington. For instance, it is obvious that the box was extended at the end furthest from the camera. Some additional signalling would have been required for the new line, the lever frame thereafter containing 30 levers, and it is certain that the original facilities would have been nothing like that generous! The extension of one slope of the hipped roof to form a covering not just for the signalman's door but for the whole landing was a typical SR touch of the period, the boxes at Exeter Central (1925 and 1927 respectively) having this feature. This box remained in use until 20th September, 1970 when, with only freight traffic remaining on the line, all points were converted to hand operation. *G.F. Gillham*

Pinhoe (1878)

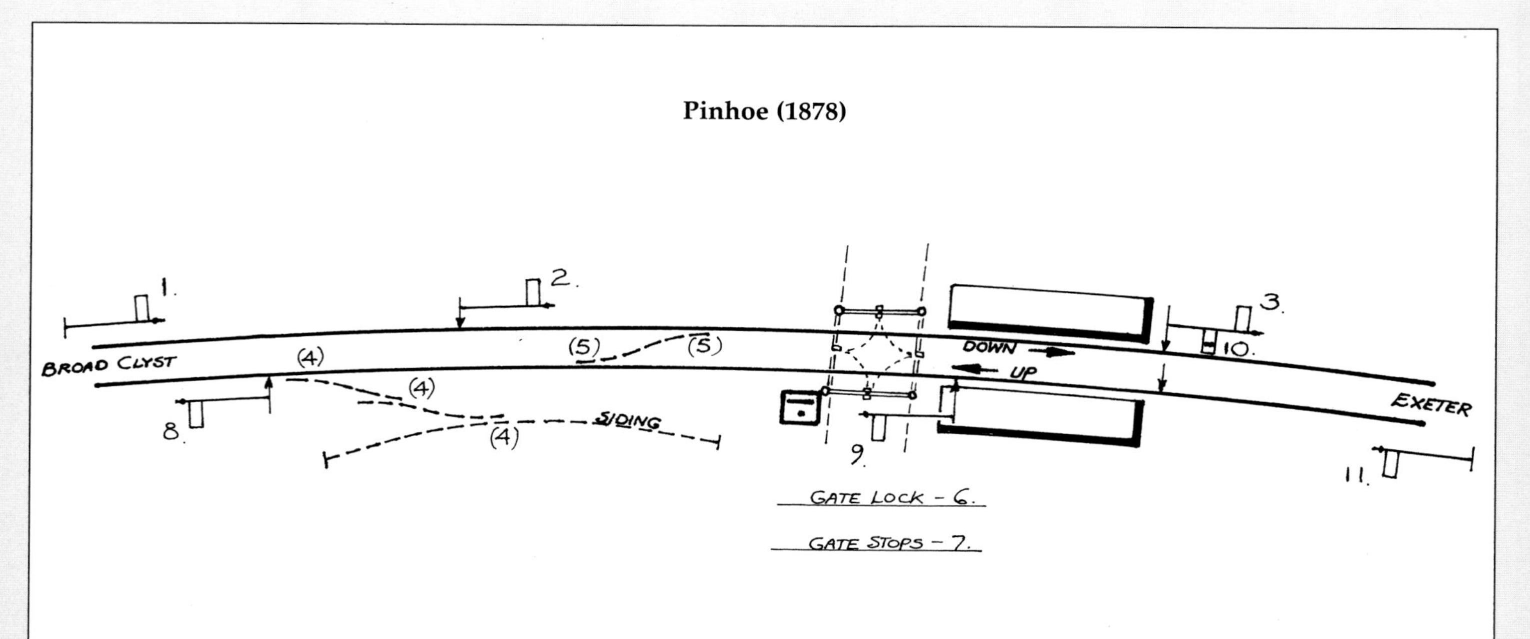

Plate 22: The simplicity of some of the type '1' boxes opened in the period 1875-1878. The diagram shows the alterations made in 1882 (dotted) for the opening of this station to goods traffic. The very minimal provision allowed this to be done without extending the frame, purely by using up the two spare levers (Nos. 4 and 5). By that time the 'Distants', Nos. 1 and 11, were fitted with fish-tail arms, but no shunting signals were thought necessary to control the new connections.

Chapter Two

The Type '1' Boxes

As explained in Chapter One, the type '1' box appeared in response to an urgent demand for signalling created by the 1873 Regulation of Railways Act which encouraged all companies to bring their passenger lines up to specific standards and furnish returns on their progress. At the time the scene was one of total disorder. Some Block Working existed, but it was patchy and did not necessarily cover a whole line, and there were quite a few interlocked signal boxes at junctions and the busier stations. Sometimes the two did not exist together, there being plenty of locations which had the Block System but no interlocking and others with interlocking that were still worked by the old methods. The average small wayside station still had its policeman to work the signals and points by isolated levers, the telegraph instruments being under the control of the station clerk. It will be appreciated that the LSWR, with a system stretching from London to Plymouth and the remotest parts of North Devon and Cornwall, had much to achieve in a very short time in order to comply with the legislation, and signal boxes had to be basic structures which were quick to erect.

Stevens & Son secured the contract for this work, and although they supplied the lever frames and other fittings it is not known whether they were responsible for the signal box design or even if they actually erected the structures. There is, however, a similarity between the type '1' box and boxes of the same period found on other railways which makes a contractor's involvement likely. Despite the haste of their construction there was no hint of jerry-building, and many of them survived for more than a century. Most of them were small, containing on average less than 20 levers, for at the time it was the company's policy to provide running signals only and leave shunting movements to be controlled by hand signal.

The type '1' box consisted of a base of brick, rubble masonry, or occasionally stone, above which the operating floor was almost entirely of timber. In its original form this woodwork consisted of vertical boarding behind large external cross-bracing timbers, with small sliding windows two panes deep set well up under the eaves. Hipped slate roofs were standard, usually adorned with a metal ventilator, and as heating in those days was universally by open hearth fires, a brick chimney stack was provided. Many of these boxes had no windows to light the ground floor, the signal engineer having to potter about in the dark when he came to do his maintenance! There was no standard height for these boxes, and they ranged from ground level to the very lofty depending on the view of his layout obtainable for the signalman. It must be remembered that in those days there were no track circuits, so a signalman needed a good clear view of everything under his control. The need for speed in building these structures could not quell the Victorian artisan's love of decoration, and the eaves were adorned with valences cut to intricate patterns. Indeed, the general simplicity of the design was much disguised by painting the main external timbers in a darker shade than the vertical boarding below, imparting something of the air of a half-timbered cottage to these boxes.

Plate 23: The two methods of lever economy practised by the LSWR to avoid the necessity of extending a signal box when additions to the signalling were made.

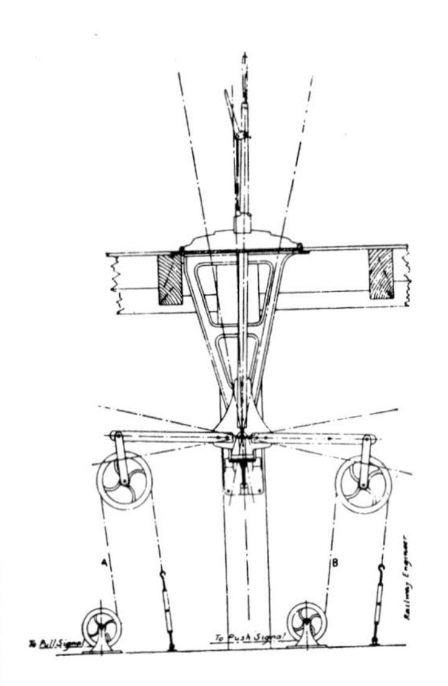

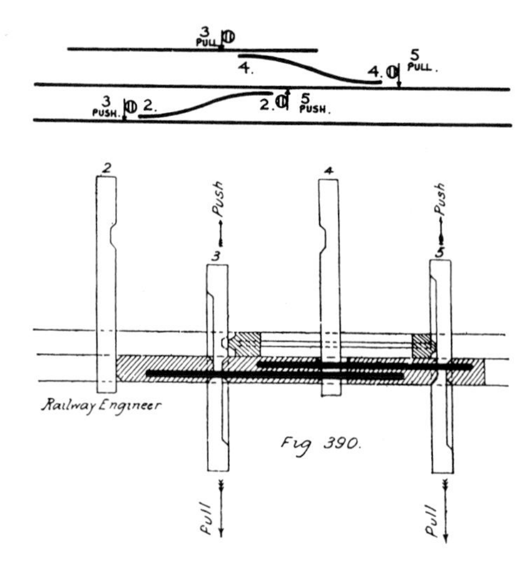

Push and Pull levers stood half-way in the frame when 'Normal', being pushed to clear one signal and pulled to clear the other. Occasionally even further economy was possible by mechanical selection so that two signals could be operated by either action, which one actually clearing being dependent on the position of the points. The right-hand sketch shows the mechanical locking necessary for these levers.

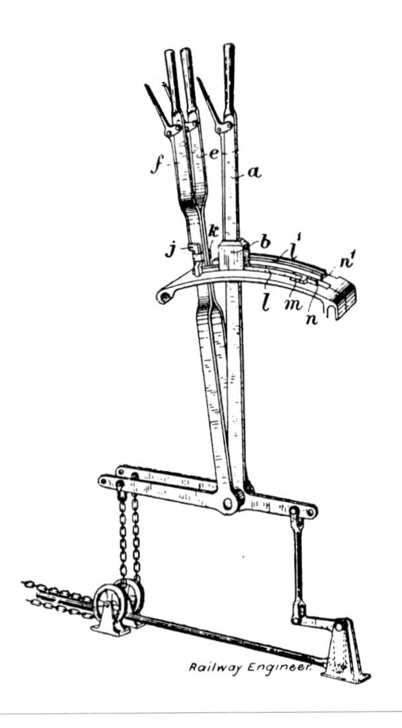

Right: 'Russell' levers as installed in an ordinary Stevens' lever frame. The lever operating the points stood slightly forward of the two smaller ones operating the shunting signals. From this drawing it will be appreciated that this type of equipment imparted a very untidy appearance to the interior of the signal box, with levers standing at all angles instead of being in a nice neat row.

The type '1A' had all these features in common, except that for some unknown reason a large box-like vent was situated in the middle of the roof. As signal boxes of the time were lit by oil lamps suspended from the ceiling, this may have been an experiment in clearing away the fumes, but the ventilation obtained from them seems to have been a little too hearty and the signalmen tended to block them up with old newspaper or cardboard. They were never very numerous, so perhaps the experiment was deemed a failure at quite an early date, although a smaller version of the wooden roof vent appeared in later designs.

The small size of the average type '1' has already been mentioned, and this was their main drawback. The lever frame, the associated shelf of instruments, and the booking desk occupied just about all the available space, and as the workforce became more demanding there was no room even for such basic necessities as a sink. Because of this, many type '1' boxes were later extended, either to provide some creature comforts for the occupant or to allow some additional levers to be added to the frame as the policy towards shunting signals changed. However, if signals were the only additions every effort was made to avoid extending the box itself, either by using 'push and pull' levers which allowed two functions to be operated from one lever or by the introduction of 'Russell' levers. The latter were the invention of E. Russell, signal superintendent at Exeter in the 1890s, and involved two small levers travelling in the same slot in the frame as the points to which the signals applied. They were used quite widely in the West Country but do not seem to have spread elsewhere on the system, and had the unfortunate effect of making the interior of the box look very untidy.

Lavatories were not provided, the signalman having to make use of the public facilities on the station during suitable gaps in traffic. At isolated boxes a separate small building containing an earth closet was erected for the signalman's convenience.

The external cross-bracing timbers of these boxes quickly proved to be a design fault, the angles formed by them creating traps for rain water which rotted the vertical boarding beneath. It has been postulated by other historians that some of these boxes were built with horizontal boarding from the start and may never have had exposed main timbers, but whilst the present author accepts this as a possibility, he considers it unlikely in view of the fact that the same method of construction was continued in the early type '2s'. Whatever the truth of this matter, by 1900 most of them had received the protective layer of weather-boarding which totally altered their appearance, and often at the same time the ornamental valences was removed. In a few cases where the decay was serious, they were bricked up to window sill level, and occasionally other materials were used such as sheet asbestos as at Fordingbridge. Many of them also lost their brick chimney stacks as combustion stoves replaced open fires, a stove-pipe chimney being substituted.

The longevity of the type '1' can be judged from the fact that most of the lines west of Salisbury, those converging on Andover and Salisbury from the South, the Mid-Hants Line, and several other places remained almost exclusively type '1' country into the 1960s, although of course none remained in their original form. There must have been many others in the London area, but these tended to be early casualties because of the constant re-modellings and widenings made necessary by ever-increasing traffic. Some boxes of this type also

Plate 24: Photographs of type '1' boxes in their original condition are fairly rare owing to their early date of modification, and where they do exist they tend to form part of a general station view rather than being a close-up study of the box itself. This picture of Dean, taken *c.*1890, has been previously published elsewhere, but no apology is offered for including it here since it shows exactly what these boxes looked like when first erected. Note particularly the cross-bracing timbers picked out in colours darker than the underlying boarding, the brick chimney stack, and the small ornamental valence around the eaves. This example dated from around 1875 and was on a brick base, but other materials were often employed. The standard type '1' windows with their sliding frames look very small in relation to the building as a whole, but afforded an adequate outlook for the signalman. Dean box lasted until 9th September, 1980, having given more than a century of continuous service, ample evidence of the quality of Victorian engineering. It contained a Stevens' frame of 17 levers, about the average size for a type '1' box.

Lens of Sutton

appeared on the Somerset & Dorset line, of which the LSWR had taken a joint lease with the Midland Railway in July 1876. The former company assumed responsibility for signalling, and many of the boxes were unmistakably 'South Western' in character, although there was a tendency for them to exhibit minor differences in detail as if to emphasise the special nature of the line.

By 1878 the initial rush to install full signalling on existing lines was over, and there was time to look more carefully at signal box design. The type '2' (*see next chapter*) which replaced it was slightly more roomy and had bigger windows. It would seem reasonable to suppose that no type '1' boxes were constructed after their introduction, but this was not the case. For instance, Brockenhurst East (1888) was a typical type '1' box, opened a full 10 years after the design had been superseded, and some new boxes of the early 1900s were similar. In some cases, such as Amesbury, this reflected the known use of secondhand woodwork and windows, and whilst this could be true of the others no positive evidence is available.

Summary of Boxes Classified as Type '1' and Type '1A'

Period of construction	1873 to 1878.
Ground Floors	Brick or rubble masonry. Some stone.
Operating Floors	Timber. Large external timbers with vertical boarding below. Later covered with outer layer of horizontal boarding.
Windows	Sliding. 2 panes deep by 3 or 4 across.
Roofs	Hipped, slated.
Height of Operating Floor Above Rail Level	Non-standard.
Stairs	External. Wooden steps and handrails.
Chimneys	Brick stacks, later stove-pipes.
Special Features	Type '1A' only - Large wooden roof vent.

Plate 25: A pre-1900 view of Downton station, showing that, even at that early date, the type '1' box had been modified with horizontal boarding. This box survived unaltered until closure of the line on 4th May, 1964, although it had been used only as a ground frame since 1st December, 1922. It contained a 12-lever Stevens' frame. *Lens of Sutton*

Plate 26: A station view that shows the original type '1' signal box almost by accident, this time at Medstead on the Mid-Hants line. This one had a window to light the locking room, a feature welcomed by the signal engineer but not provided on a regular basis in boxes of this type. Unfortunately the chimney stack is just out of the picture, but the external timbers, hipped slate roof, and small valence are typical. This box contained a 15-lever Stevens' frame, and survived in modified form until 23rd January, 1967. *Lens of Sutton*

Plate 27: One of the type '1' boxes originating from the 1873 Regulation of Railways Act, seen here in the standard modified form with the cross-bracing timbers covered with horizontal boards. Often when these boxes were modified the valences were removed, but in this case they were left in place. The relieving arch over the lead-off bed was a most unusual feature. Chandlers Ford box contained a 15-lever Stevens' frame (2 of which were push and pull), and was abolished on 22nd May, 1969 after a period of disuse.

G.F. Gillham

Plate 28: A view of Bracknell, *c.*1900, showing the slightly different type '1' box with its cross-bracing timbers exposed. Standard boxes of this type had slate roofs, but this one had a roof of boards covered with tarred canvas secured by battens at a slightly steeper pitch. As all the other features seem to be standard, it is reasonable to suppose that this roofing was original rather than being a later modification, but the reason for it is obscure. Perhaps the rash of signal box building in the 1870s had created a shortage of slates! This box was also unusual for a type '1' by being of all-timber construction.

Lens of Sutton

Plate 29: Bracknell box as it appeared in 1970, showing one of the ways in which type '1' boxes were modified to protect the timber framework. In this example vertical boarding has been used instead of the more usual horizontal boards, and the valence has disappeared as it did in most cases where these buildings were modified. The original small central window which lit the locking room had been replaced by a couple of hatches which could be opened as required by the maintenance men. The roof does not seem to have been altered since the time of the previous photograph, even the small non-standard metal vent having survived. Bracknell box was taken out of use on 27th January, 1974.

John Scrace

Plate 30: Station staff pose for the photographer on the platform at Witley, and in the process provide us with a tantalising glimpse of the signal box, which dated from 1876, in its original condition. Compare this with the photograph below. *Lens of Sutton*

Plate 31: Witley box as modified. The saw-tooth valence has gone and the timbers have been enclosed with vertical boarding, but the locking room window seems to be unaltered. Is it an optical illusion caused by the different methods of construction, or has the operating floor actually been lowered? Certainly the box looks taller in the earlier picture. The extension to the porch houses the signalman's toilet -a refinement unheard of at the time the box was built, and an unusually generous provision for a type '1' box sited on a station platform. Normally the signalmen would have been expected to use the station facilities during convenient intervals in traffic. Although the chimney of the box is not visible in the original view it was almost certainly a brick stack, but with the modifications came the combustion stove and attendant stove-pipe. The metal roof vent is of an early pattern, and may have survived from the original 1876 structure. This box contained a 17-lever Stevens' frame, and was closed on 19th December, 1973. *John Scrace*

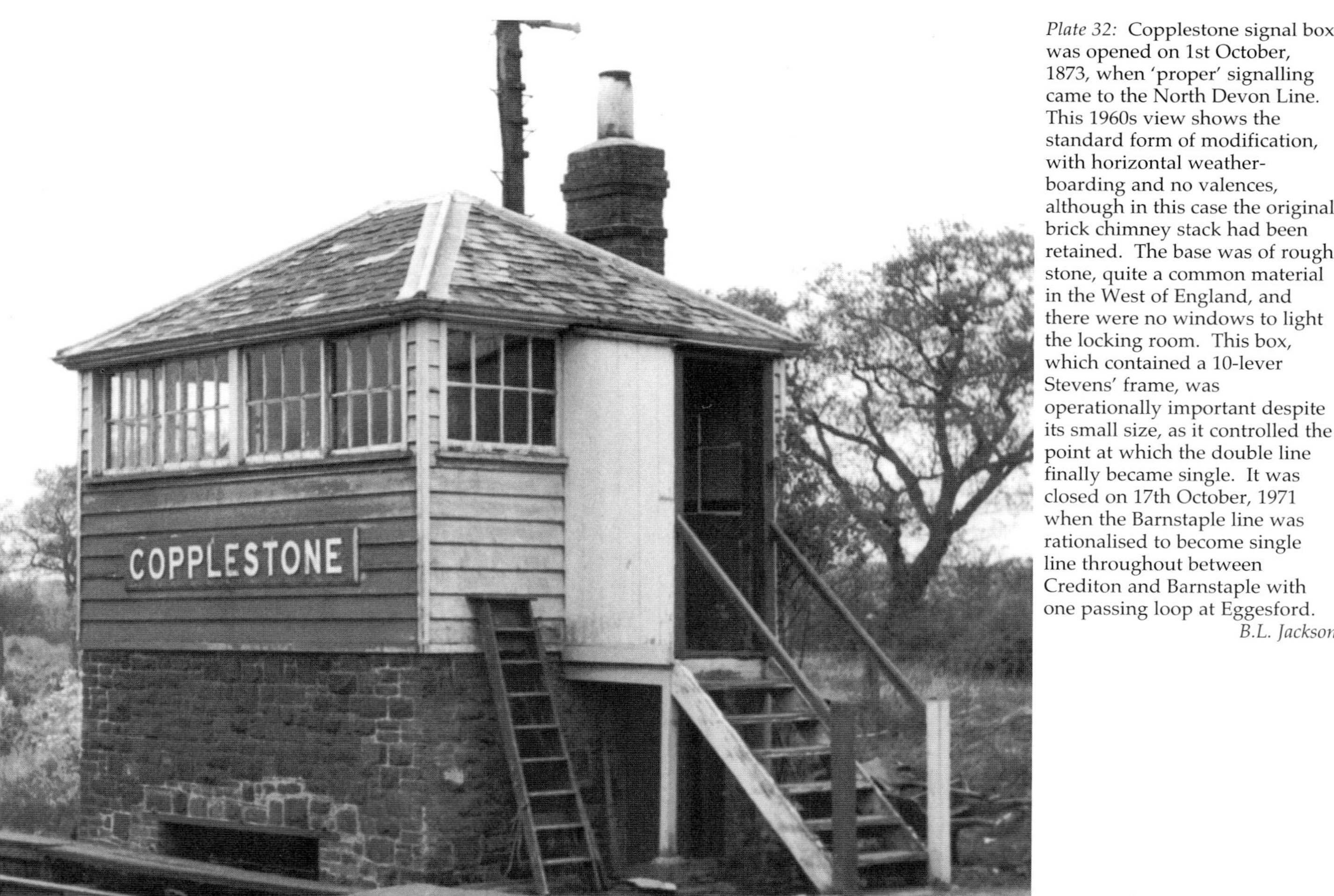

Plate 32: Copplestone signal box was opened on 1st October, 1873, when 'proper' signalling came to the North Devon Line. This 1960s view shows the standard form of modification, with horizontal weather-boarding and no valences, although in this case the original brick chimney stack had been retained. The base was of rough stone, quite a common material in the West of England, and there were no windows to light the locking room. This box, which contained a 10-lever Stevens' frame, was operationally important despite its small size, as it controlled the point at which the double line finally became single. It was closed on 17th October, 1971 when the Barnstaple line was rationalised to become single line throughout between Crediton and Barnstaple with one passing loop at Eggesford.

B.L. Jackson

Plate 33: This box at Gillingham (Dorset) dated from the general signalling programme for the West of England main line carried out in 1875, and is seen here in the standard modified form. The rough stone base is slightly taller than usual, which emphasises the small dimensions of the operating floor. Note the standard LSWR roof vent, a feature not often present in type '1' boxes. The interior presented a very cramped appearance, the original 16-lever Stevens' frame being augmented with no less than 14 'Russell' levers in 1894 when shunting disc signals were provided. When the box was replaced by a modern structure on 28th April, 1957 the signalmen must have heaved sighs of relief!

B.L. Jackson Collection

Plate 34: Chard Junction, a typical type '1' box of 1875 vintage after the usual modifications, except that the brick chimney stack has survived. The roof vent is of the early 'chimney' pattern instead of the standard LSWR model depicted in the previous photograph. Like many boxes on this line, the base was without windows and was constructed of rubble stonework. It contained a 15-lever Stevens' frame and gate wheel, and lasted long enough to control the single-line layout and colour-light signals introduced by the Western Region in 1967. However, by 1980 the building was found to be unstable, and it was closed on 11th September, 1982 when a temporary switch panel took over its functions pending the opening of a permanent panel on 11th December that year. *C.L. Caddy*

Plate 35: This picture merits inclusion here not only because it provides a close-up study of the woodwork of a typical modified type '1' box but also because pictures of this location are very rare. Hardington, which stood between Sutton Bingham and Crewkerne, was unique amongst boxes of this type in having a Saxby & Farmer lever frame with levers at 5-inch centres, originally of just 6 levers. When sidings for milk traffic were provided in 1909 this was increased to 8 levers. This view, which shows signalman David Pettitt on duty, also reveals a non-standard valence which might have been original, but rather suggests that it was cut down by having the 'points' sawn off at some stage, although it is difficult to imagine why anyone should go to that much trouble! The milk sidings were abolished in February 1937, but the box survived as a simple block post until 1959.

Mike Clements Collection

Plate 36: Fordingbridge illustrates another, and less attractive, way of covering up the external timbers of a type '1' box - with asbestos panels. Several boxes were treated in this fashion, although the reason is obscure. Perhaps there was a shortage of timber at the time! In this example the brick chimney stack has given way to the stove-pipe, and an additional window frame appears to have been inserted in the end nearest to the camera. This box originally contained a Stevens' frame of 11 levers (including one push-and-pull) to which one was subsequently added. It lasted until the closure of the West Moors to Salisbury line on 4th May, 1964.

B.L. Jackson

Plate 37: In some cases the woodwork of type '1' boxes seems to have reached an advanced stage of decay before remedial action was taken, and there was then little alternative but to brick up the whole building to window sill level. This course of action was demonstrated at Bow (Devon), where the newer brickwork contrasted sharply with the original rubble masonry of the base. Despite the fact that money was obviously spent on this 1873 box, the open hearth fireplace and brick chimney survived. The box had a 12-lever Stevens' frame. It was seldom open in its final years, and was finally abolished on 26th January, 1964.

B.L. Jackson

Plate 38: Although some buildings erected for other purposes were occasionally converted to signal boxes (*see Totton, Plate 18*) it was rare for them to make use of any standard designs in the conversion. Here at Dunbridge, a perfectly standard type '1' top was erected on part of the roof of what was once a crossing keeper's cottage, the interlocking being housed in the original sitting room. The remainder of the building then became virtually disused, although the permanent way gang stored some equipment there. This example demonstrated the usual modification with horizontal weather-boarding, but retained the brick chimney. The 'torpedo' roof vent was a somewhat unusual feature. The box enjoyed a long life, not closing until 17th October, 1983. It had originally contained a Stevens' frame of 18 levers and a gate wheel, this being extended to 21 levers in July 1915 in connection with alterations to the layout.

M.J. Tattershall

Plate 39: Whilst most type '1' boxes were small, there were examples of larger structures. Sidmouth Junction was not only longer than average (it contained a 31-lever frame), but also considerably loftier. Examination of the picture reveals it to be an all-timber type '1' box mounted on a high brick base, in effect making it three storeys high. The original valences and brick chimney stack survived, but unusually for a box of this size, there were no roof vents. For some unknown reason, one of the locking room windows had been boarded over! This box closed in connection with the singling of the line to Exeter on 21st May, 1967. *A.E. West*

Plate 40: There were a number of boxes which were basically type '1s' but which, because of site difficulties, could not be erected in the normal way and therefore appeared to be different. There were some in the London area, where lack of lineside space dictated the adoption of 'overhead' structures, but the reason here at Fremington is perhaps less obvious. The platform was very narrow with sidings behind it serving a riverside wharf, and one wonders why the box was not erected on the opposite platform where there was more room. The result of the decision to site it on the up platform was a unique type '1' edifice with over-sailing top on a tall, narrow, brick base, with windows on all four sides to afford the occupant a view of the shunting taking place on the quay. The large brick chimney stack appears to have been shared with the fireplace in the adjoining waiting room. The height was necessary, in those days before track circuits. to allow the signalman a clear view the points at both ends of the crossing loop, the whole layout being on a slight 'S' bend. Fremington box had a 14-lever Stevens' frame, and was closed on 3rd November, 1968.

C.L. Caddy

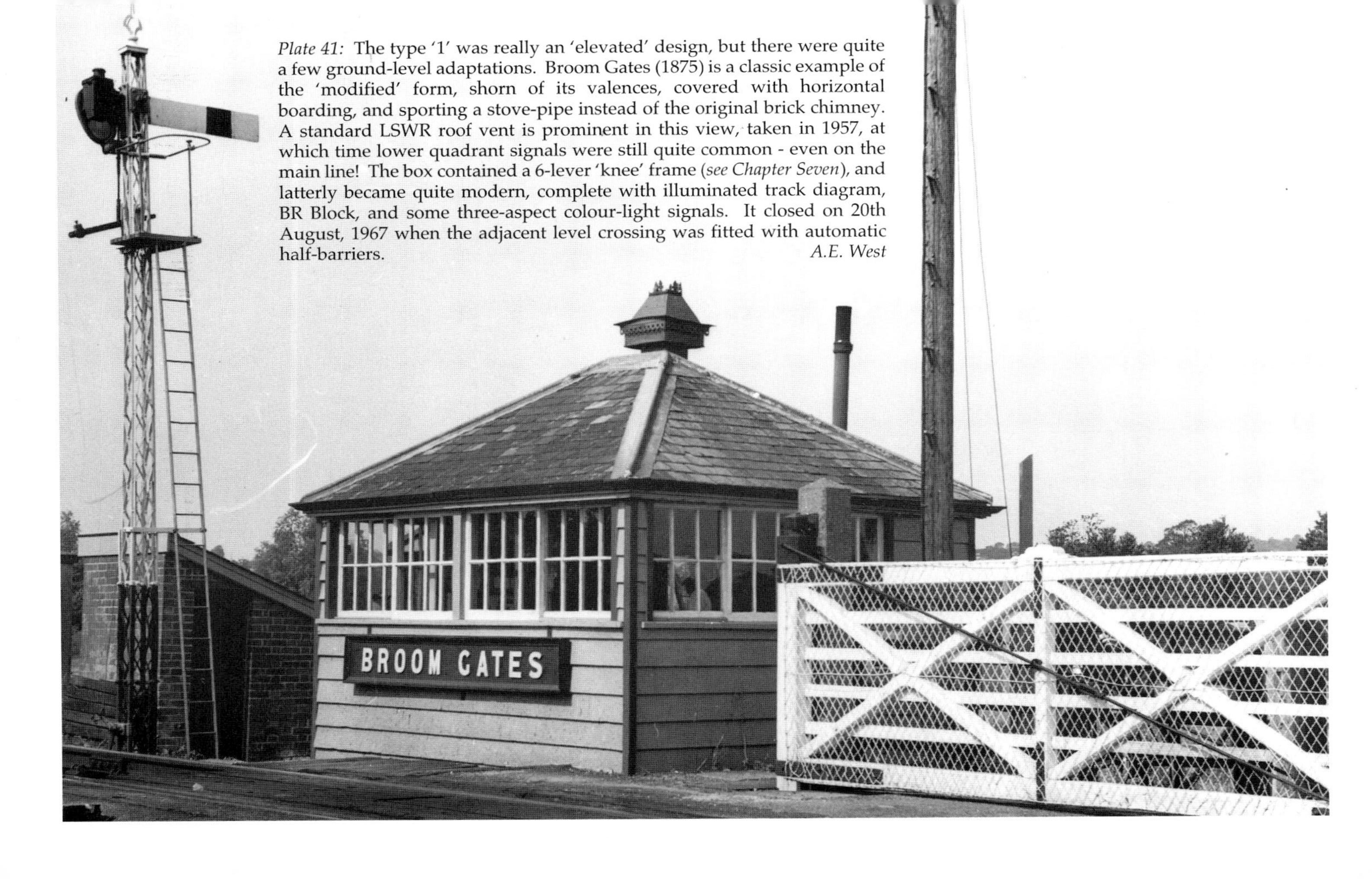

Plate 41: The type '1' was really an 'elevated' design, but there were quite a few ground-level adaptations. Broom Gates (1875) is a classic example of the 'modified' form, shorn of its valences, covered with horizontal boarding, and sporting a stove-pipe instead of the original brick chimney. A standard LSWR roof vent is prominent in this view, taken in 1957, at which time lower quadrant signals were still quite common - even on the main line! The box contained a 6-lever 'knee' frame (*see Chapter Seven*), and latterly became quite modern, complete with illuminated track diagram, BR Block, and some three-aspect colour-light signals. It closed on 20th August, 1967 when the adjacent level crossing was fitted with automatic half-barriers. *A.E. West*

Plate 42: Scale drawing of Broom Gates signal box, a typical ground-level type '1'.
South Western Circle

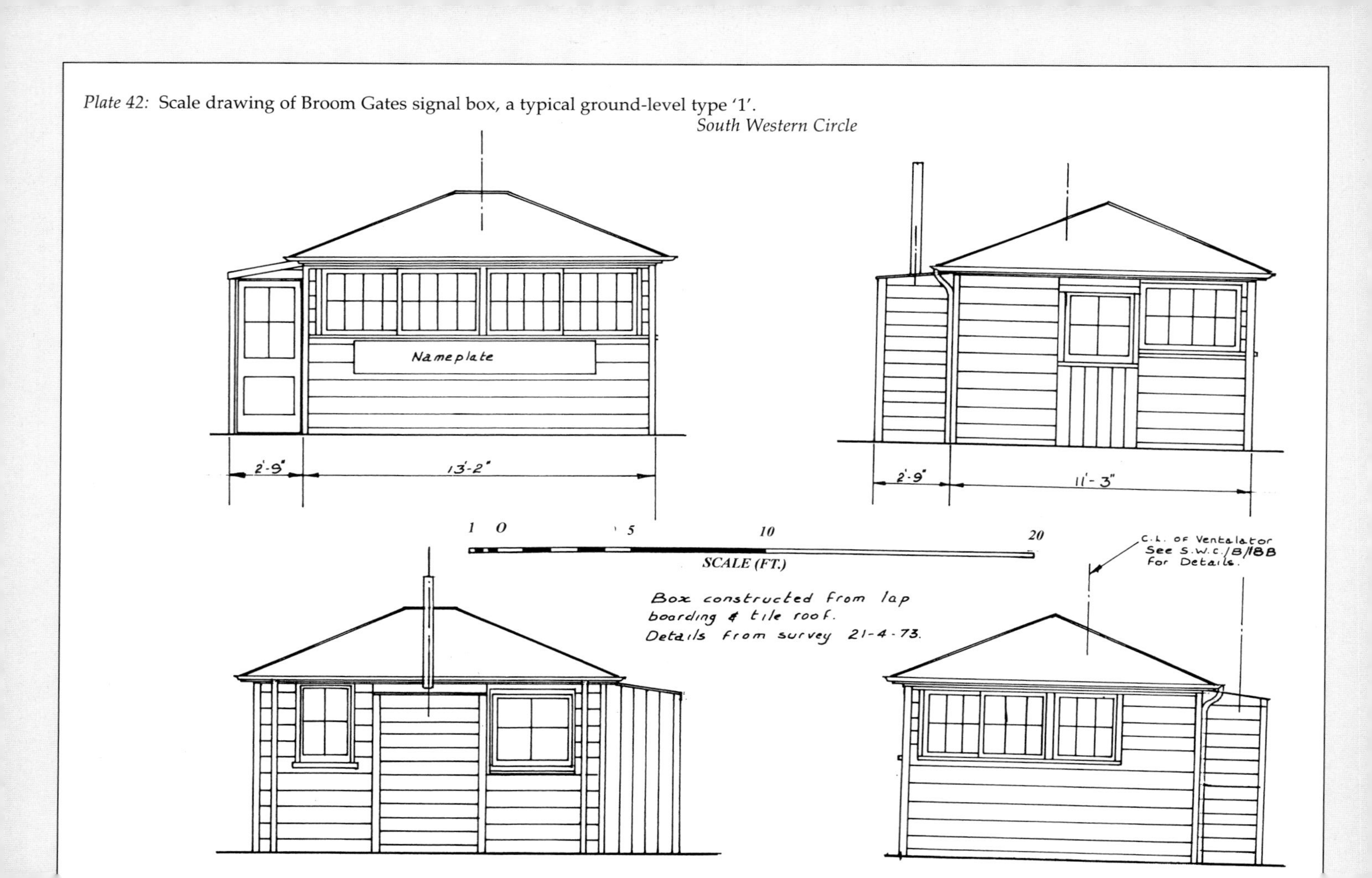

Plate 43: A rather poor-quality photograph of Ottery St Mary, showing the old ground-level type '1' signal box. This one had been modified to a slightly lesser extent than Broom Gates (previous picture), the valence being retained. It contained a 14-lever 'knee' frame, and was replaced by a brick box of early BR design on 20th November, 1955.

Lens of Sutton

Plate 44: Braunton Gates box (actually only a ground frame) demonstrates the use of secondhand materials. It was opened in 1889 in connection with the doubling of the Ilfracombe line, at which time Braunton station received a new signal box, the roof, woodwork, and windows of the original one being re-used here. A brick wall rendered with cement was built up to window sill level, and the old material fixed on top of it. Because it was a re-cycling of an old structure instead of being purpose-built it was much larger than necessary. A box of that size could have easily accommodated a frame of 16 levers, but a little 'knee' frame of 5 levers, three of which were spare, was all that it contained. It remained in use until closure of the line on 5th October, 1970.

Pamlin Prints

Plate 45: The branch to Amesbury was not opened until 1901, and it would therefore seem an unlikely location for any type '1' signal boxes. However, Amesbury box consisted largely of materials salvaged from the old box at Grateley where a type '4A' structure was provided to contain the experimental low-pressure pneumatic equipment. This re-used material, complete with some of the valence, forms the part of the box nearest to the camera. Additions were made in 1906 when the line was extended to Bulford, so the far end of the structure was built on afterwards. Because the same materials and style of windows were used in this extension, the exact point at which the new meets the old is not readily apparent. In this extended form it contained a 'knee' frame of 25 levers, a modest size achieved by the absence of shunt signals and the provision of an 18-lever ground frame to control the Bulford end of the station. A layout of the same complexity, fully signalled, would have required about 70 levers, but the Amesbury line was officially a 'Light Railway' which allowed things to be done on the cheap! The line was closed to all traffic on 4th March, 1963.

B.L. Jackson Collection

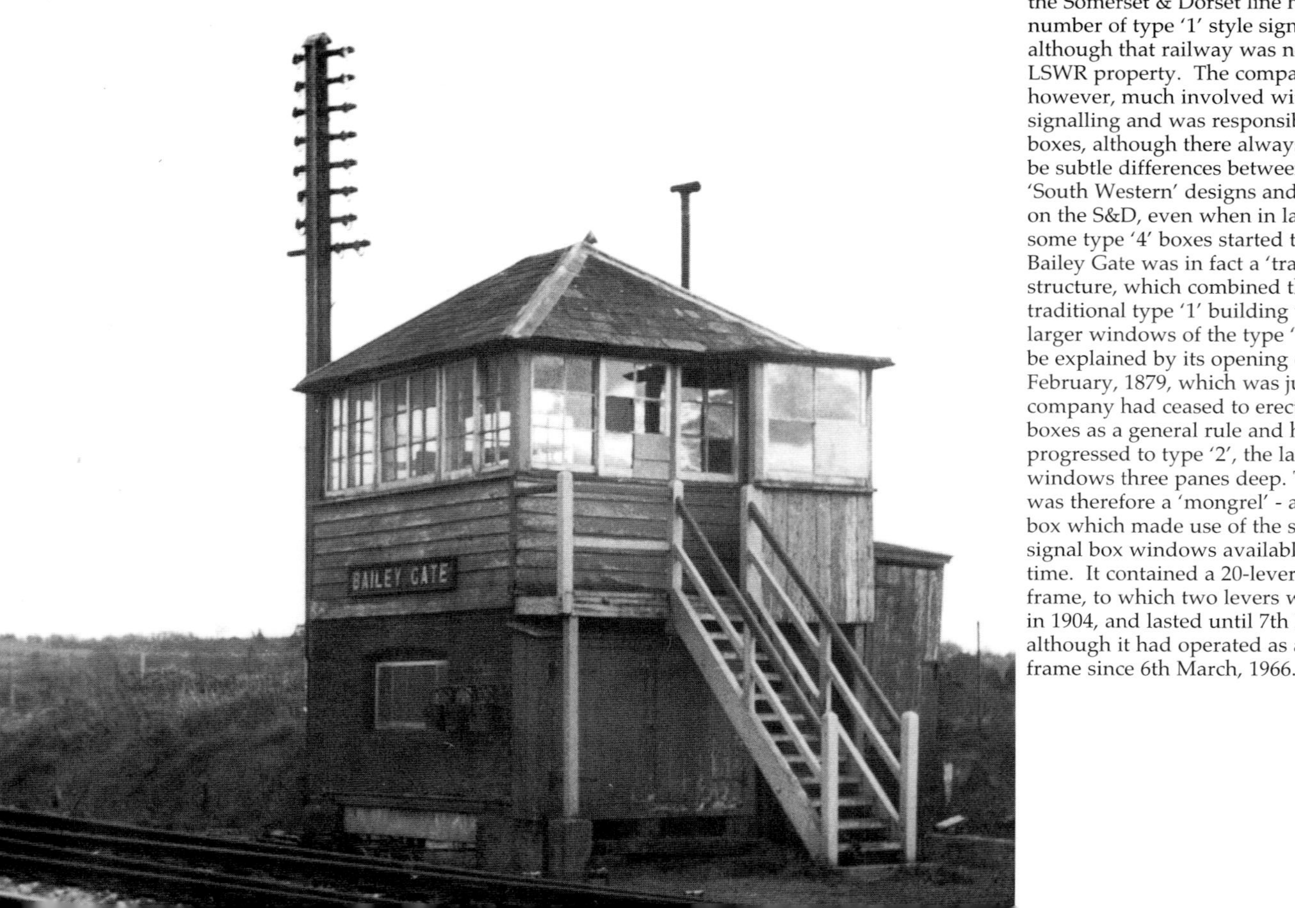

Plate 46: As mentioned in Chapter Two, the Somerset & Dorset line had a number of type '1' style signal boxes although that railway was not strictly LSWR property. The company was, however, much involved with the signalling and was responsible for the boxes, although there always seemed to be subtle differences between standard 'South Western' designs and those used on the S&D, even when in later years some type '4' boxes started to appear. Bailey Gate was in fact a 'transitional' structure, which combined the traditional type '1' building with the larger windows of the type '2'. This can be explained by its opening date, 10th February, 1879, which was just after the company had ceased to erect type '1' boxes as a general rule and had progressed to type '2', the latter having windows three panes deep. This box was therefore a 'mongrel' - a type '1' box which made use of the standard signal box windows available at the time. It contained a 20-lever Stevens' frame, to which two levers were added in 1904, and lasted until 7th May, 1968, although it had operated as a ground frame since 6th March, 1966.

B.L. Jackson

Plate 47: As signalling became more sophisticated it was often necessary to add levers to the original frames, and whenever possible this was done by extending the existing signal box rather than building a new one. Ringwood demonstrates an example of this, the extension being at the far end of the building. The neatness of the 'join' is such that the work is only detectable by the twin locking room windows being off-centre. This is thought to have been done in 1904 when the adjacent level crossing was provided with a gate wheel and six levers were added to the frame, although there were further signalling alterations in 1929 which increased the number of levers from 25 to 32, and it is possible that the extension was carried out then. This box was reduced to ground frame status, solely to control the gates, on 5th September, 1965, complete closure following on 8th January, 1967. *C.L. Caddy*

Plate 48: The Sidmouth branch was opened in 1874, so this type '1' box formed part of the original fixtures and fittings. It was somewhat taller than average for a box of this type, which made it an interesting structure in itís own right, but it is included here to illustrate the smallest extension that could be made to a box, a matter of just a couple of feet. The 'new' part was cantilevered out from the end wall farthest from the camera, but it is not known when this was done or why. Perhaps the box simply became too cramped for the comfort of the signalmen when the Tyer's tablet machine was installed, the original method of working being Train Staff and Ticket. It contained a 23-lever Stevens' frame (2 being push-and-pull), and lasted until the closure of the line to all traffic on 8th May, 1967.

R.C. Riley

Plate 49: Some extensions were considerable. Yeovil Junction 'B' had a 26-lever frame installed in 1909 in connection with the re-modelling of the station, and this must have filled up the original structure wall-to-wall. To allow the signalmen some basic comforts this additional section was added to the operating floor. On 4th July, 1914 this box suffered the indignity of being knocked down the embankment by a derailed train (*see Plate 148*), but it was soon resurrected with very little change in appearance. It was closed on 30th April, 1967 as part of the Western Region's singling scheme

Author's Collection

Plate 50: This fascinating view of Exmouth Junction not only shows what was perhaps the ultimate extension, which virtually doubled the size of the 1875 box, but also allows us to see a century of evolution in the design of signal boxes. The original box (nearest the photographer) contained 25 levers, but in 1927 the SR enlarged the layout with a new engine shed and additional marshalling sidings, extending the frame to 49 levers. The brickwork of the extended base contrasts sharply with the old stone section. Even the brick chimney stack survived this upheaval! It is difficult to understand why the railway company elected to take this course of action, since the cost of extension can have been little less than that of building an entirely new box, and the disruption to the working of traffic much more severe. It was eventually replaced by the new BR box (to the right of the picture) on 15th November, 1959, and this photograph was taken soon after the changeover.

Alan Postlethwaite

Plate 51: Built concurrently with the type '1s' were a few '1As', almost identical but distinguished by large, box-like roof vents that seemed rather out of scale with the dimensions of the signal boxes. This box at Holmsley was modified only to the extent of having its external timbers covered with horizontal boards, the valences and brick chimney being allowed to remain. Exactly why the designer of these boxes thought that a building so small and never occupied by more than one man at a time needed that degree of ventilation, which was of course additional to that available by opening the windows, is inexplicable, and the roof ventilators, which were fitted with internal wooden shutters worked by ropes and pulleys, were little more than an annoying source of draught which the signalmen tended to cure by inserting old rags, cardboard, or other materials. The design was never particularly widespread, but several examples survived into the 1960s. Although seldom switched into circuit latterly, Holmsley box remained serviceable until the Ringwood line was closed on 4th May, 1964. It contained a 13-lever Stevens' frame. *C.L. Caddy*

Plate 52: Horsebridge was another type '1A' box. In this case the modifications were more whole-hearted than at Holmsley. The valence has gone and, although not visible in this picture, the brick chimney has been replaced with a stove-pipe. The large square roof vents certainly dominated this kind of box. Horsebridge box was switched in for only two short periods each day, mainly to deal with the pick-up freights, but in June 1964 the sidings were abolished and the box stood unused until the line closed on 7th September that year.

Oakwood Press Collection

Chapter Three

The Type '2' Boxes

The 1873 Act had brought about a rush of signalling work which enabled the company to supply the Board of Trade with reasonable progress returns, but after five years the company felt they had reached a point where they could look more carefully at the design of signal boxes. There was still much work for the signal engineers and contractors as new lines were being opened, new connecting spurs put in, and layouts enlarged to accommodate the ever-increasing traffic, but the urgency had largely been removed from the situation. The type '2' box was the result of this slightly more relaxed approach, and was almost certainly the work of somebody within the LSWR organisation. As a design it lasted for just seven years - 1877 to 1884 - and was therefore not very widespread. It did, however, represent considerable advances on the original type '1s'.

From the signalmen's point of view, perhaps the most significant improvement was an increase in workspace with larger windows which produced a less gloomy interior, but although type '2' boxes were somewhat more roomy than their predecessors there were still no lavatories, and facilities were pretty sparse. The windows, which took up most of three sides of the box, had sliding frames three panes deep by two or three across, the former seeming the more common, and a railed walkway was sometimes provided in front of them to facilitate cleaning, but this was omitted where the structure was very close to the track. The ground floors were of plain brick, without recesses and usually with one central window to light the locking room, above which rose timber-framed structures covered with vertical weather-boarding - although there is some evidence that originally these boxes had external cross-bracing timbers in the manner of the type '1s'. One curiosity was the provision of toplight windows that were totally useless, hidden as they were beneath ornamental saw-tooth valence boards. The buildings were topped with a hipped slate roof, little wooden spike finials adorning each end of the ridge. These tended to be rather fragile, and they were usually missing in later years. For the first time there seems to have been a standard height for signal boxes of 8 feet above rail level, a standard that was followed for all subsequent designs unless the siting was exceptionally difficult and called for special structures. Most type '2' boxes were fitted with combustion stoves and therefore had stove-pipe chimneys rather than the brick stacks of the type '1s'.

A few type '2' boxes were built wholly of timber, Weybridge (horizontal boarding) and West Byfleet (vertical boarding) being good examples. In the wooden structures the locking room windows tended to be left untouched, but many of the others had them bricked up as an anti-blast measure in World War II.

In 1878, just a year after the introduction of the type '2' box - the company produced a drawing entitled 'Ascot and Aldershot Line Standard Boxes'. Why the standard design was deemed unsuitable for this new line was not explained, but a special architectural style, classified as 'Type 2A' came into being.

Plate 53: A rather nice period view of Feltham West box, taken around 1900. Note the spike finials at each end of the roof ridge and the stove-pipe chimney. The toplight windows are totally obscured by the valences, which in this case are cut to a somewhat more intricate pattern than usual. Because of the tight clearance between the building and the down line the railed walkway in front of the windows is omitted. This box lasted, with only minor alterations, until the adjacent crossing was fitted with lifting barriers under CCTV surveillance and placed under the control of Feltham Panel on 10th January, 1975.

Lens of Sutton

Although, in theory, this was a 'standard' design (the drawing office said as much), there were a number of variations on the main theme. For instance, Ascot Branch box was entirely of wood whereas all the others had brick ground floors, but they did all share some common features. These included hipped slate roofs and sliding windows with frames containing two panes across by three down, together with top-lights largely obscured by the saw-tooth valences as in the ordinary type '2s'. In fact, from this description the two sound more or less identical, but the visual affect was surprisingly different. The wooden version at Ascot was almost in a class of its own, but belongs to the '2A' group by virtue of it being one of the batch erected for the opening of the line.

Signalling remained quite basic, few, if any, shunt signals being provided, so the average size of these boxes was small. Diagrams of the time show discs to control some movements but nothing to control others which would appear to be equally attended by risk, so the basis on which such decisions were made is a mystery. Many boxes of this type contained push-and-pull levers to control the few shunt signals that were provided, but these would seem to be later additions.

Type '2' and '2A' signal boxes were mainly confined to London and the outer suburban area, although they did manage to spread as far West as the upper half of the Portsmouth Direct Line, and consequently their survival rate has not been high. At the time of writing (1999) just one - Bollo Lane Junction (Acton) - survives, and even this has lost its lever frame and contains a miniature panel. The type '3s' which superseded them in 1884 perpetuated some of their features.

Summary of Signal Boxes Classified as Types '2' and '2A'

Period of Construction	1877 to 1884
Ground Floors	Brick. Windows to locking room provided. A few all-timber versions known.
Operating Floors	Timber. Vertical matchboarding below windows. Originally had external cross-bracing timbers.
Windows	Sliding. Each frame 3 panes deep by 2 or 3 across (type '2') or 3 deep by 2 across (type '2A').
Roofs	Hipped, slated. Wooden spike finials at ends of ridge. Latter feature type '2' only.
Height of Operating Floor Above Rail Level	8 feet (standard).
Stairs	External. Wooden steps and handrails.
Chimneys	Stove-pipe.
Special Features	Railed walkway provided around outside of windows except where close to line (type '2' only).

Plate 54: Sunningdale was typical of the type '2s' found in the outer suburban area. This one had valences of a more standard pattern (compare with previous picture), but even when viewed from ground level the toplight windows were virtually invisible. There is evidence that this box originally had external support timbers in the manner of the type '1s', but they were enclosed with vertical boarding many years ago. The spike finials are missing in this 1964 view, but they were fragile and often became broken long before the boxes closed. This box was also very close to the track, and therefore had no walkway in front of the windows. It closed on 5th September, 1975 when control of the crossing was transferred to Feltham Panel.

JohnScrace

Plate 55: This view of Grove Park Crossing, taken in May 1974, shows a type '2' box with the front section of valence missing and exposing the toplight windows. There has also been a somewhat half-hearted attempt at removing the walkway, part of the decking remaining in place whilst the handrails are missing! The locking room window has been bricked up, probably an anti-blast measure from World War II. This demonstrates the ways in which a perfectly standard type of building can be mutilated to the extent that it almost escapes classification.

John Scrace

Plate 56: The type '2s' never spread farther out from London than the Portsmouth Direct line. This example at Liphook dates from the doubling of that section of line in 1877, making it one of the earliest of its type. Its early date could explain the subtle differences in either the valences or window frames which are apparent when comparing this box with the standard version, and which allow the toplights to be partially exposed to view. On the other hand, when passing the new down sidings for use in April 1899, the Board of Trade Inspector complained about the 'very indifferent view of the line' available to the signalman from this box, which stands close to an overbridge (immediately behind the photographer). The LSWR agreed to move the structure closer to the down line, and if this was done some alterations might have taken place at the same time. It contained a 20-lever Stevens' frame, and closed on 16th February, 1975.

B.L. Jackson

Plate 57: Liss, also on the Portsmouth Direct, was a rather more standard type '2', although the vertical boarding was replaced by wooden panels. Note that the spike roof finials, although broken off, are still visible. This box dated from 1878, although the wooden extension nearest to the level crossing housing the signalman's toilet was a much later refinement. Compare this picture with the previous one (Liphook), and the differences become obvious. Here the toplight windows are totally obscured by the valences in true type '2' style. Liss also contained a 20-lever frame, and closed on 16th February, 1975. *John Scrace*

Plate 58: The last surviving type '2' box, Bollo Lane Junction (Acton). In this instance the railed walkway in front of the windows remains intact, as do the spike finials and valances. The only alteration would seem to be the glazed extension nearest the camera containing the level crossing controls, doubtless added when road traffic increased and the signalman's view of approaching vehicles became inadequate. This box now contains a small panel instead of the lever frame.

Plate 59: Type '2' boxes could look very different when shorn of their valances, as this large example at Walton-on-Thames shows. Originally 'Walton West', it appears to have been opened in 1882 in connection with the additional up line between Weybridge and Surbiton, at which time it contained 38 levers. Later this was extended to 46 levers, but the building itself does not carry any evidence of extension. In this guise it looks very much like a type '3', but the date of construction is too early and the window frames, 3 panes deep by 2 across, give away its true identity, as does the plain brick base without recesses. One has to imagine the valences covering the toplight windows to gain any impression of how this box looked in original form. It was closed on 22nd March, 1970. *John Scrace*

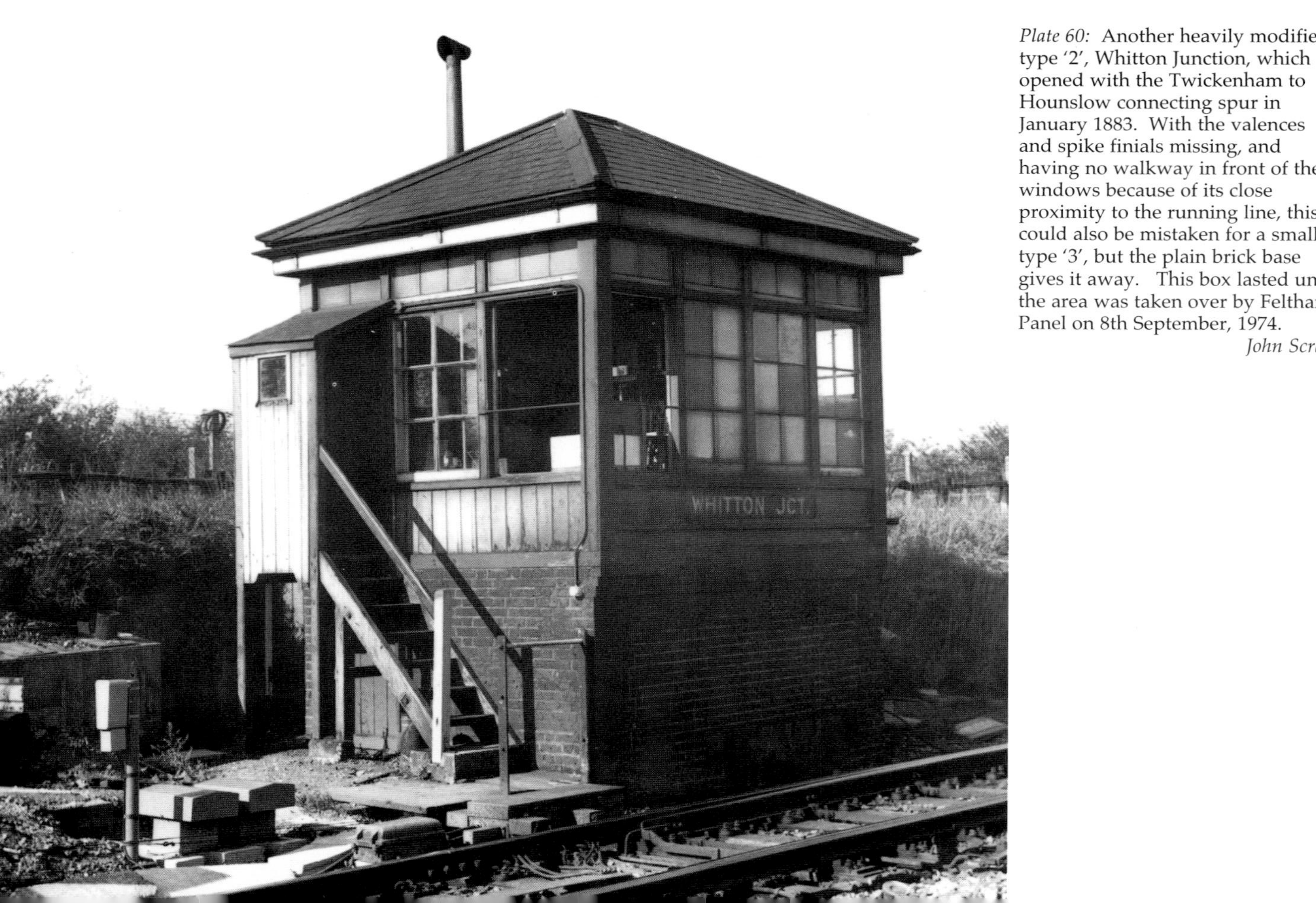

Plate 60: Another heavily modified type '2', Whitton Junction, which opened with the Twickenham to Hounslow connecting spur in January 1883. With the valences and spike finials missing, and having no walkway in front of the windows because of its close proximity to the running line, this could also be mistaken for a small type '3', but the plain brick base gives it away. This box lasted until the area was taken over by Feltham Panel on 8th September, 1974.

John Scrace

Plate 61: Very few type '2' boxes were built wholly of wood, but Weybridge, dating from 1882, provided a rare example. The boarding is horizontal throughout, and the building is quite tall to enable the signalman to see over trains passing on the two down running lines to the points in the bay line and dock sidings. Here again the structure has been much modified, the valences and finials being removed, and the provision of locking room windows was unusual for a type '2'. The lever frame held 68 levers, making this box one of the largest of its kind. It closed on 22nd March, 1970 when control of the area came under Surbiton Panel.

John Scrace

Plate 62: The previous plate (Weybridge) shows that rarity, the all-timber type '2' box, with horizontal boarding, but in some it was done vertically as here at West Byfleet. From these two views and other evidence, it would seem that windows in the locking room were only provided in the wooden versions of type '2' boxes, the standard pattern having unbroken brick bases. Here again all the 'trimmings' have been removed. A 35-lever frame was installed, and the box survived until 22nd March, 1970.

Plate 63: As explained in Chapter Three, in 1879 the LSWR designed a different 'standard' box, classified '2A', for the lines around Ascot and Ash Vale. The usual hipped-roof was modified to the extent that the length of ridge was negligible, and there was less woodwork between the brick base and window sills. Otherwise the old type '2' features were perpetuated, including the toplight windows obscured by valences and the vertical boarding. Frimley Junction, opened with the line in June 1879, contained a 28-lever frame, and lasted until the area was placed under the control of a small panel in Ash Vale box on 25th March, 1973. The wooden structure in the foreground was a platform from which the signalman could collect the tablet for the single line section to Ash Vale. Note that the locking room window has been bricked up. *John Scrace*

Plate 64: Another '2A' box on the same line, Bagshot. For some reason the bottom row of window panes along the front have been painted over, but otherwise it is was a good example of the type. The standard LSWR metal roof vent is prominent in this view. The box contained a 20-lever frame, and normally switched into circuit only for the morning and evening peak services. It was abolished on 3rd July, 1973.

John Scrace

Chapter Four

The Type '3' Boxes

The year 1884 ushered in a period of instability in the matter of signal box design, the type '3' having no less than three variations before it was eclipsed by the type '4' in 1894. The earliest type '3s' were similar to the type '2s', except that the windows became much larger. They were now four small or three large panes deep, reaching down almost to floor level, and to facilitate cleaning them a railed walkway was provided around the outside in most cases - although this was omitted where the structure was particularly close to the track. As with the type '2s', the operating floor consisted of a timber frame covered with vertical match-boarding, the space between the top of the brick base and the window sills being similarly filled. As a general rule type '3' boxes did not have ornamental valences, the toplight windows being unobstructed, although one example (Petersfield) did have them, and they survive to this day! Hipped slate roofs were standard, but now without the little spike finials. The wooden box-like roof vent, like that used more than a decade earlier in the type '1As' reappeared in a smaller and less obtrusive form, but sometimes it was removed in later years. In fact, many of those type '3' boxes erected after 1890 seem to have had 'torpedo' vents instead. In the standard '3' the windows in the end walls extended the full width of the building, except perhaps for a small boarded area in one end where the combustion stove stood, and those occupying island sites with tracks on both sides (as in the 'V' of junctions) had windows all the way round. A slight modification - the '3A' - had short sections of brick wall or boarding between the windows and the back wall of the box, as at Branksome, probably because the standard window frames would not fit exactly into the width available for the building. Combustion stoves were now general, and stove-pipe chimneys were fitted.

The brick bases had recesses, two or three bays according to the length of the building, an arched locking room window being central in each bay. If signalmen had appreciated the extra space afforded by the type '2s' they must have been happier still about the type '3s' which were even more roomy! The smaller ones were virtually square in plan, which made for a lot of floor space. Quite a large number were constructed, the 1880s being a time of considerable expansion in the railway system. For instance, the 'New Line' to Bournemouth (1888) was entirely fitted out with type '3' boxes. Type '3' boxes were also used on the North Cornwall Line, which took nine years (1886-1895) to battle its way across the barren country between Halwill and Wadebridge. Over that period the design seemed to mutate slightly, the boxes on the earliest section, from Halwill to Launceston, being recognisably standard of the type whilst those to the west of Launceston showed some interesting local variations.

For some unaccountable reason, 1889 saw the adoption of a completely different type '3' box - the '3B' - with much less glazing. These were plainer in style, the top-light windows being discontinued. The windows now consisted of sliding frames, four panes down by 3 across, in sets of two, each set being divided by a fixed upright. The spaces between the top of the brickwork and the window sills and the top of the windows and the unadorned eaves were filled with horizontal boarding. Slate hipped roofs and stove-pipe chimneys remained standard, and there was usually a small lean-to porch protecting the signalman's door. There is no evidence that the '3Bs' ever carried any roof vents except the metal variety of either standard LSWR design or of the 'torpedo' type.

There was one more adaptation of the type '3' design in which the central section of the front windows was replaced by an area of horizontal boarding and the square wooden roof vent made a return appearance. Never very numerous, these have been classified as '3Cs'. Redbridge, Southampton West, and Hamworthy Junction were good examples of this type. The latter survives at the time of writing (1999), but minus the roof vent and with replacement window frames which tend to make it look completely non-standard.

If the Type '3' era appears to demonstrate some indecision on the part of the company over the best design for signal boxes, the signal engineer seems to have been likewise dogged by uncertainty. For the most part Stevens & Son were still providing the fixtures and fittings, but latterly they became somewhat overwhelmed with work and other manufacturers were sometimes used, although the lever frames were always to Stevens' pattern irrespective of the supplier. What did vary from place to place was the level of signalling. At some boxes ground signals were provided to control every shunt movement, but at others there were none or very few. In the latter case their provision still appeared to be as random as it had been with the Type '2' boxes. Push-and-pull levers, originally seen as a cost-effective way of adding signals to a layout without lengthening the frame, were often now employed in new boxes as a means of reducing the length (and therefore the cost) of the building, but again they were not a universal provision. Block instruments remained of the Preece type, although in the late 1890s some of the busier lines were equipped with Sykes' 'Lock and Block', and this system was also favoured where there was an intermediate siding operated from a ground frame. Various patterns of Tyer's tablet machines were employed on single lines.

It was also during the type '3' years that the white light in semaphore signals to denote 'proceed' was replaced by green, this change being completed by 1893. The fact that the white light lasted so long reminds us how dark the countryside must have been at night for much of the 19th century, but the gradual spread of better lighting made a white signal lamp very difficult to spot from the footplate of an engine.

The company seems to have grown tired of continually changing designs for signal boxes, and it is almost as though somebody had been tasked to sit down, think hard, and come up with something of lasting merit. Whether this was so or not, 1894 saw the emergence of the type '4', a design so stylish and practical that it was to last for the rest of the LSWR's days and actually be used (with a few minor adjustments) by the new Southern Railway in some of its early schemes. Despite the availability of this smart new design, the box erected at Lymington Junction in 1915 was unmistakably a type '3', which shows how difficult it can be to date a box from its architectural style.

The survival rate of type '3' boxes has been quite high, several remaining in the Bournemouth area and one at Petersfield at the time of writing. The '3Bs' have not been so lucky, as most of the lines on which they were provided have either been closed or reduced to the 'basic railway' without any signalling. Only Bere Alston survives in a derelict state.

It is interesting that although the company had built up quite a collection of standard box designs by the beginning of the 19th century they still felt the need to produce the occasional 'one off'. Newton Tony (1915), on the Amesbury branch, is a classic example of waywardness in this respect, the design owing nothing to anything erected previously, even the specified materials being unusual for such work.

Summary of Boxes Classified as Type '3' & '3A'

Period of Construction	1884 to 1897 (With occasional later examples).
Ground Floor	Brick, with recesses and locking room windows. Some all-wood examples, usually with vertical boards.
Operating Floor	Timber. Vertical boarding below window sill.
Windows	Sliding, large, with top-lights. Frames either 3 or 4 panes deep by 3 or 4 panes across. In '3A' only, windows did not extend to full width of building at each end.
Roofs	Hipped, slate.
Height of Operating Floor Above Rail Level	8 feet.
Stairs	External, with wooden steps and handrails. Small porch over signalman's door.
Chimneys	Stove-pipe.
Special Features	Railed walkway around windows (sometimes omitted) and large roof vents.

Summary of Boxes Classified as Type '3B'

Period of Construction	1889 to 1892.
Ground Floor	Brick (some recessed) with arched windows to locking room.
Operating Floor	Timber. Horizontal boarding above and below windows.
Windows	Sliding, in sets of two frames each containing 4 panes down by 3 across, each set divided by wooden upright.
Roofs	Hipped, slate.
Height of Operating Floor Above Rail Level	8 feet.
Stairs	External, with wooden steps and handrails. Porch over signalman's door.
Chimneys	Stove-pipe.
Special Features	Design localised.

Summary of Boxes Classified as Type '3C'

Period of Construction	1890 to 1897.
Ground Floor	Brick, with recesses and windows to locking room.
Operating Floor	Timber. Horizontal boarding.
Windows	As for Type 3B, except central section of front window area replaced by horizontal boards.
Roofs	Hipped, slate, with small wooden roof vent.
Height of Operating Floor Above Rail Level	8 feet.
Stairs	External, with wooden steps and handrails. Small porch over signalman's door.

Plate 65: Petersfield is the only type '3' box known to have been fitted with decorative valences, which (surprisingly) survive to the present day. Originally this box almost certainly sported a wooden roof vent which was removed at some stage, perhaps when the building was re-roofed. Note that the windows are much larger than in the previous type '2s', reaching down almost to floor level. This, plus the toplights, gave the signalman an awful lot of glass to clean, and generally he was assisted in this task by the provision of a walkway with handrails all around the windows. However, here there was insufficient clearance between the up line and the building. The roof profile on this box is a little unusual, almost giving the impression that the building was widened for some reason. With a frame of 52 levers, Petersfield ranked as one of the larger type '3' boxes and controlled quite an extensive layout which included the junction with the Midhurst branch. However, modernisation has totally altered the interior, only a few levers from the middle section of the frame remaining in use to control a crossover and associated signals whilst the main line running is worked from a switch panel. *C.L. Caddy*

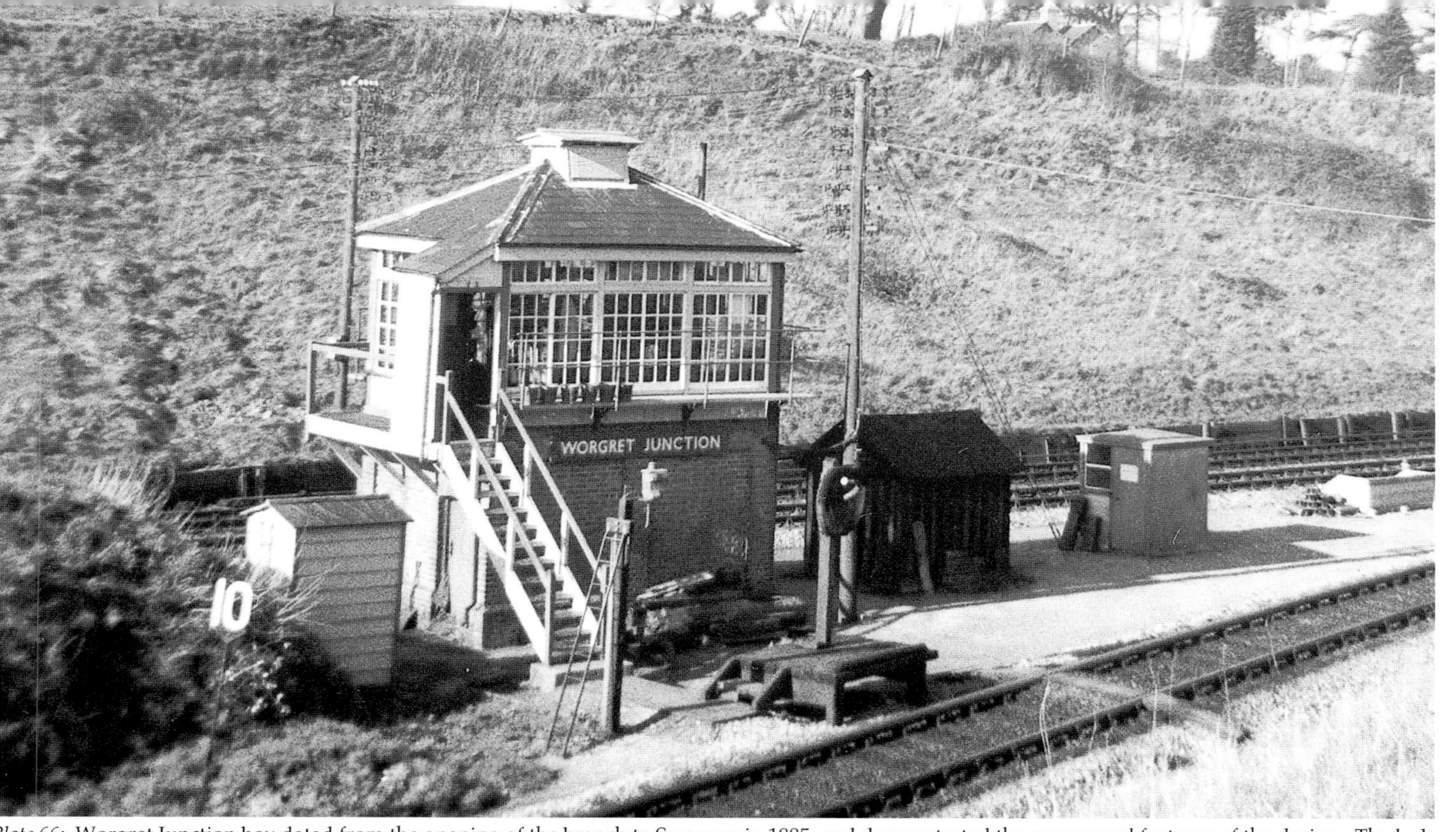

Plate 66: Worgret Junction box dated from the opening of the branch to Swanage in 1885, and demonstrated the more usual features of the design. The lack of valances emphasised the amount of glazing, which was even more generous than usual at this location because the box stood in the 'V' of the junction and had windows on all four sides! The square wooden roof ventilator was a standard provision for type '3' boxes, as was the railed walkway in front of the windows unless a box was dangerously close to the track. This box contained a Stevens' frame of 16 levers, and lasted until 23rd May, 1976 when its function was transferred to a ground frame.

B.L. Jackson

Plate 67: The new line to Bournemouth of 1888 was entirely equipped with type '3' boxes, this one at Sway being a classic example. The wooden roof vent had been removed by the late 1950s, but otherwise it remained little altered until closure on 26th February, 1967. The recessed brickwork around the arched locking room windows is very plain in this view. The box had a 17-lever Stevens' frame.

M.J. Tattershall

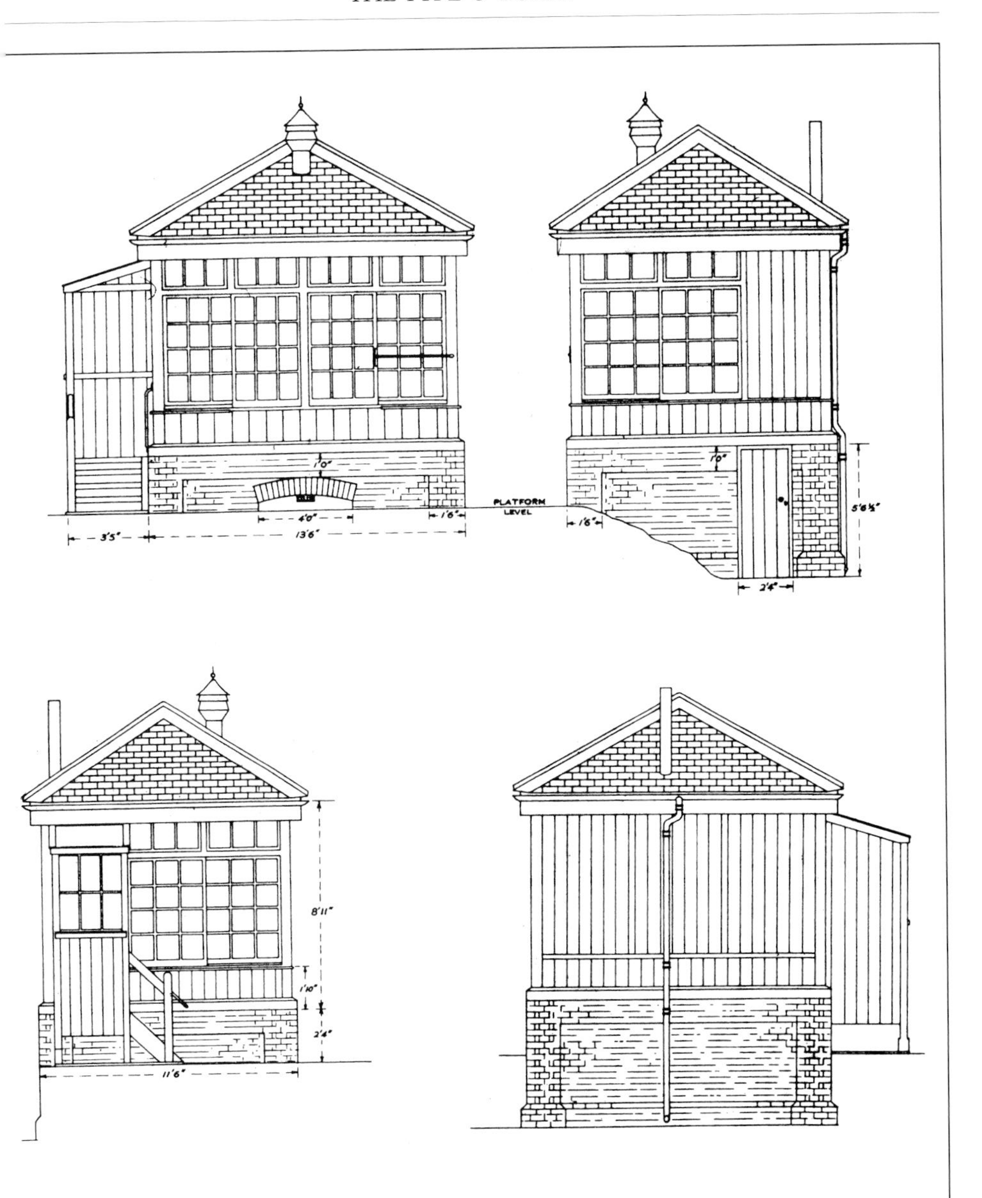

Plate 68: Detail drawing of the platform-level type '3' box at London Road, Guildford. In many respects this box was similar to Sway (*see previous page*), but the height of the building was somewhat less. Because of this no railed walkway was provided in front of the windows, which could be easily cleaned from the platform with the aid of a pair of steps! This was one of the type '3s' which had a 'torpedo' roof vent instead of the large wooden variety.

South Western Circle

Plate 69: Fullerton Junction box was opened in 1885 in connection with the new line between that point and Hurstbourne, and apart from the absence of the roof vent, was a typical type '3', complete with recessed brickwork and railed walkway. It contained a 28-lever Stevens' frame, and survived until closure of the Andover to Romsey line on 7th September, 1964. For the last four years of itís life it was opened only 'as required', which, judging by its condition, was not very often!

B.L. Jackson

Plate 70: Not many type '3' boxes exhibited obvious signs of extension, but Fratton East certainly did! It opened in June 1885 with a 38-lever frame, but this was later extended to 47 levers which required the lengthening of the building. The additional section can be detected at the left-hand end by the unequal bay in the brick base containing a smaller locking room window. There was no attempt to 'centre' the roof vent! This box was taller than the general run of type '3s' to afford the signalman a clear view of the shunting movements going on in the yard. The layout is on a curve, and a building of standard height would have given a very imperfect view of all the pointwork. Portsmouth panel box took over the area on 7th April, 1968, both boxes at Fratton being closed. *John Scrace*

Plate 71: Fratton Yard was another of the 1885 type '3' boxes to be found in the Portsmouth area, and controlled the level crossing over the East Southsea branch plus a connection to the engine shed. The branch was closed in 1914, but 'Yard Box' lingered on as a block post until 7th February, 1932 when it became a ground frame with little function except to control the gates, this part of the old line being incorporated into the EMU depot. By the time this picture was taken in 1968 it had lost its name board, but was otherwise virtually unaltered. It was finally abolished in July 1969. This box contained a 16-lever frame, many of which were spare latterly.

John Scrace

Plate 72: Stockbridge was another typical type '3'. The opening date is uncertain, but it would appear to date from the doubling of the line in 1885. It contained a Stevens' frame of 16 levers, and like Fullerton Junction *(Plate 69)* lasted until closure of the line on 7th September, 1964 although mostly switched out latterly. *B.L. Jackson*

Plate 73: Not a good quality picture, but who could resist this rare shot of Test Gates box, near Redbridge! Note that the windows are non-standard, being only three panes deep instead of the usual four, and it is tempting to suggest that some surplus type '2' fittings were used. The box dated from November 1885, and controlled the busy level crossing carrying what was then the main road into Southampton from the West. After World War I road traffic began to show a marked increase, and the line was bridged a few yards south of this box which was closed, together with the level crossing, on 18th November, 1930. No signalling diagrams have come to light so the number of levers in the frame is unknown, but they would not have amounted to more than ten. *Railtrack*

Plate 74: Launceston was built as a fairly standard type '3' box for the opening of the line from Halwill in 1886. At that time it contained an 18-lever frame, but as a staff economy during World War I it was agreed to close the GWR box which controlled that company's adjacent station and install a separate lever frame of 16 levers in the LSWR box, thus enabling one signalman to control both stations on a 'shared cost' basis. This work was brought into use on 10th August, 1915, and to accommodate the GWR's frame and instruments the building was doubled in width and given matching windows in what was the back wall. This naturally involved an entirely new roof, so if a wooden roof vent was originally provided it was doubtless removed at the time. A walkway to assist window cleaning was not thought necessary here, as the box stood on the station platform and it was probably just as easy to use a pair of steps for this task. This box lasted until the end of the North Cornwall Line on 3rd October, 1966. *B.L. Jackson*

Plate 75: As explained in Chapter Four, the North Cornwall Line was so long in the building that the standard type '3' design began to show some interesting local variations, perhaps because a local contractor was employed instead of the railway's own Civil Engineering Department. Tresmeer, opened in July 1892, demonstrated some subtle differences, although the basic type '3' features are unmistakable. It is obvious that at some stage the boarding below the window sills suffered from decay and was replaced by six courses of bricks, perhaps not surprising in this wet and windy part of the Country, but apart from that there were few , if any, alterations. An interesting feature was the brick steps instead of the usual wooden flight. The number of crossing loops on this line were reduced in the mid-1960s as an economy measure which, unfortunately, failed to save it, Tresmeer box being abolished on 14th November, 1965. It had a 17-lever frame. *B.L. Jackson*

Plate 76: Another 'North Cornwall' type '3' - Camelford - opened in August 1893. As at Tresmeer, the woodwork beneath the windows has been replaced by a few courses of bricks, but here the base is of stone, and obviously at one time contained a large arched window to light the locking room. One wonders why it was bricked up. In the London area this was often done as an anti-blast measure during the last war, but this would hardly have been a consideration in this remote area. Perhaps the glass had a tendency to get broken by milk churns or parcel trolleys being moved around on the platform. This box also had steps built of brick instead of the usual wood. Like Tresmeer, Camelford contained a 17-lever frame, but it managed to survive as a crossing place until closure of the line on 3rd October, 1966.

Alan Postlethwaite

Plate 77: The extended type '3' box at Eastleigh West, opened in 1883 as 'Bishopstoke West' with a frame of 85 levers. The opening date was in fact one year before the type '3' box was introduced as a 'standard' so either it was then an experimental design which the company liked and subsequently adopted or it was much modified at a later date. It became 'Eastleigh West' in 1899 when the station was also renamed. Unusually for such a large box there was no square wooden roof vent, one of the 'torpedo' type being provided instead. The extension dated from 1905, when the frame was lengthened to 90 levers plus an additional small 'routeing' lever. Originally the recessed brick base of four bays had a locking room window in each, but they were bricked up during the war. This box closed on 6th November, 1966, when a new panel box was opened at Eastleigh. *A.E. West*

Plate 78: The type '3B' box was introduced in 1889, and although quite a number were built they tended to be 'bunched' in certain localities. One area where they appeared was in and around Plymouth, to which city the LSWR obtained independent access in 1890. The box at Bere Alston was part of this scheme, and demonstrates all the classic type '3B' features. The toplight windows have been discontinued, the area under the eaves being occupied by horizontal weather-boards. The main sliding window frames continued to be four panes deep as with the previous type '3s', but the panes were wider and almost square. Boxes of this type were never fitted with either ornamental valences or wooden roof vents, although some had ventilators of the 'torpedo' type. The lean-to porch seems to have been a standard fitting. Bere Alston is an example of the 'West Country' version of these boxes, in which the base walls were plain, without recesses. Type '3B' boxes in other areas had the recessed brickwork of the type '3s'. This box originally contained just 17 levers, increased to 30 in 1927 when it took over the work formerly done by the separate Branch box which controlled the Callington line. Although the building shows signs of extension at the end farthest from the camera, it hardly seems enough to accommodate a frame almost twice the size of the original, so perhaps the box was uncommonly spacious in its early days. It was replaced by a 2-lever ground frame on 7th September, 1970, but remains in a derelict condition at the time of writing (1999). *Hugh Davies*

Plate 79: There were very few '3B' boxes in the London area, Wimbledon Park (1889) being one of them. Note that, away from the West of England, the brick base had recesses, the central one containing an arched window (bricked up) to the locking room. A 'torpedo' roof vent was fitted, together with a stove-pipe chimney, and there was a lean-to porch of slightly different construction from the one at Bere Alston. The box contained 19 levers, two of which were push-and-pull, and lasted until 1997.

John Scrace

Plate 80: The much-extended Shawford Junction, photographed in the early 1960s. The box opened in 1891 with a 20-lever frame, but in 1931 its area of control was greatly extended by the closure of Shawford Station box and the introduction of four roads thence to Eastleigh. In connection with this work another 10 levers were installed, and the necessary extension to the building is evident at the end farthest from the camera. This again was a standard '3B' structure, with recessed brick base, lean-to porch, and hipped slate roof complete with 'torpedo' vent. The Southampton-Winchester-Fareham area was another in which boxes of '3B' pattern were once quite common, but all have now been closed. Shawford Junction itself was abolished on 6th November, 1966. *R.C. Riley*

Plate 81: Ground-level version of the type '3B' at Stoney Bridge Crossing on the Ilfracombe line. Apart from the absence of a ground floor for the locking, it was exactly the same as 'elevated' boxes of this class. It was opened in 1889, and contained a 6-lever 'knee' frame. The crossing was hand operated, so there was no gate wheel. Closure came when the line itself was closed on 5th October, 1970.

B.L. Jackson

Plate 82: Some ground-level type '3Bs' were erected, mainly at level crossings, Heddon Mill (on the Ilfracombe line) provides an example. It also shows how the appearance of a building can be considerably altered simply by changing the window frames! In this view, taken in 1968, the second and fourth sliding frames are original, but the other two are of a recent pattern. The bungalow building behind the box was the crossing keeper's cottage. This was one of those boxes which controlled a level crossing and yet could 'switch out' as a signal box, the gates and signals being worked by a crossing keeper at times of light traffic. It contained an 8-lever 'knee' frame, and the gates were hand operated. It also closed on 5th October, 1970.

A.E. West

Plate 83: In 1890 another variety of type '3 'box appeared, classified as '3C'. The general structure, including the window frames, was very similar to that of the type '3Bs', but there was a return to box-style wooden roof ventilators. The main difference in these buildings was that the central section of window space was blanked out with an area of horizontal boarding, foreshadowing the type '4s' that followed them. Hamworthy Junction was opened in 1893 to replace the old 'Poole Junction' box, and it originally contained 56 levers to which 3 were added in 1901 without any need to extend the structure. This view, taken in 1952, shows it more or less 'as built' complete with wooden roof vent. *R.C. Riley*

Plate 84: A close-up view of Hamworthy Junction box taken in 1968, by which time the roof vent had been removed and a toilet for the signalman had been provided in the little hut on the platform. Later the windows were all renewed with larger panes which made the building seem totally non-standard, and that is how it remains at the time of writing. *C.L. Caddy*

Plate 85: Fulwell Junction Box opened in 1895, making it one of the earliest type '4s'. The neat and tidy nature of the design is obvious in this view which, although taken as recently as 1970, shows it in virtually original condition. Note especially the curved upper window frames, a small detail but one which gave these boxes much of their appeal. Being situated in the London suburbs, the twin locking room windows had been bricked up as an air raid precautions measure, but this seems to be the only disfigurement. Like all type '4s' this one had a stove-pipe chimney, the cowl on which is just visible above the ridge of the hipped roof. The lean-to porch was another standard feature of these boxes. This box contained a 23-lever frame, and remained in use until the area came under the control of Feltham Panel on 9th November, 1974.

John Scrace

Chapter Five

The Type '4' Boxes

There is a touch of genius about the type '4' signal box which allows what is basically a very plain structure to become handsome solely through its proportions and attention to detail. Coming off the drawing board in 1894, it represented an entirely new approach to signal box design. Up to that time there had been a pre-occupation with giving the signalman a virtually unobstructed view by surrounding him with glass, but for the first time it seems to have been realised that most of the windows behind the lever frame were rather a waste because any view from them was obstructed by the block shelf and associated instruments. With sound common sense, the designer grouped the windows where they were of greatest value, at the front corners.

This reduction in window area enabled the (by then) traditional practice of building the operating floor mainly of timber to be discontinued, and most type '4' boxes were of brick right up to eaves level. In a very few cases the structure was entirely of timber (as at Bentley and St Cross) and there were rare stone examples, but brick was the usual material.

The windows were very distinctive, being made up of sliding frames each of which held four panes of glass. The frames of the upper panes were attractively curved at the tops. Between the top of the window frames and the eaves was a row of hopper-type ventilator panels. Arched windows, sometimes one centrally, lit the downstairs locking room. Hipped slate roofs were continued, except for a few examples erected on the Somerset & Dorset Joint line which had gable ends. The stairs were the usual external wooden variety, but for the first time full-width landings were provided at the top of them as standard fittings, the section outside the signalman's door being enclosed by a small porch. Heating was by combustion stove (two stoves in large boxes) with the attendant stove-pipe chimney(s) , and steel roof vents were fitted.

Type '4' boxes came in all sizes, and some of the larger ones had windows in the central brick pillar. The design became very widespread, to the extent that there was hardly a line on the LSWR system that did not have at least one example. The turn of the century was still a time of railway expansion, and there were many layout improvements and re-signalling schemes which called for new boxes. The regular Type '4' had windows only at the front corners, the back wall being plain brick. This was not very suitable for locations where there were tracks on both sides of the box, so a slightly modified version, the '4A', with windows in all four corners - was developed.

The '4B' omitted the central brick pillar altogether but retained the curved-top window frames. It has been stated elsewhere that this variation was reserved for larger boxes, but this is not so. The little ground-level structure at Holme Crossing (near Wareham) which dated from 1917 and contained a mere 6 levers was a type '4B'! It was this version that was often employed later by the Southern Railway, who also came up with two other slight variations which are classified as SR '11A' and '11B' and are beyond the scope of this book.

Plate 86: The Meon Valley line, which connected Alton with Fareham, was a late arrival on the railway scene, not opening until 1903. It was laid out on a lavish scale for a line through such a rural area, and although single track throughout, was intended to be seen as offering an alternative through route between London and Portsmouth, although it was never used as such. This line and the Basingstoke and Alton Light Railway were in fact 'blocking' lines to keep the GWR out of Portsmouth, and their traffic was always meagre. All the stations were equipped with large type '4' boxes of a standard size, of which Tisted is an example. It contained a 23-lever Stevens'-type frame. All traffic ceased between Farringdon Goods and Droxford on 7th June, 1955, and the box was closed.

Norman Simmons

It is somewhat curious that LSWR type '4' boxes were to be found on two railways that were not, strictly speaking, parts of that company's system, the Somerset and Dorset Joint (S&D) and the Midland & South Western Junction. This can be readily explained in the first instance because the S&D was operated jointly by the LSWR and Midland Railways, the former taking responsibility for signalling matters. However, many of the type '4s' on this line had non-standard features, as though the company was trying somehow to make the point that this line was different. On the other hand the Midland & South Western Junction Railway (MSWJR) was never operated by the 'South Western', and at the Grouping actually found itself in GWR ownership, so the only connection must have been through Sam Fay, a former LSWR man who became General Manager of the line from 1892 to 1899. Fay maintained an excellent relationship with his former employers during this time, and no doubt arranged to 'crib' the drawings when the need arose for new signal boxes. Unlike those on the S&D, the MSWJR specimens at Ludgershall, Perham, Tidworth, Grafton South Junction, Swindon Town, and Rushey Platt were pure type '4'.

With the type '4' box came a total re-think of signalling standards, and for the first time ground signals were provided to control every movement. Indeed, the company went from one extreme to the other, the previous lack of subsidiary signals giving way to a multiplicity of ringed arms and discs. Some use was made of push-and-pull levers, but generally the lever frames in type '4' boxes were much longer than those installed in earlier designs. Stevens & Son remained the contractor, although latterly many of these boxes were supplied with Stevens' pattern frames manufactured by Tyer or the Railway Signal Co. The Block equipment was mainly Preece's, although by this time there was quite a lot of Sykes' Lock and Block in certain areas.

Despite their widespread use, there are very few boxes of this type remaining open today. Perhaps the best example is at Haslemere, but others can be found at Aldershot, Farnham, Farncombe, Poole (the former 'B' box) and Wareham, although the latter is an SR structure dating from 1928 and is unusual in that it only appears as a true type '4' when viewed from the back. From the lineside it looks like a '4B'!

Summary of Boxes Classified as Type '4'

Period of Construction	1894 to 1923. Some use after this date by SR.
Ground Floors	Brick, without recesses. Arched windows to locking room.*
Operating floor	Brick to eaves level.*
Windows	Sliding wooden frames with curved upper panes. 4 panes per frame. In front corners only, divided by central brick/stone pillar. Type '4A' *only* has windows in all four corners. Type '4B' *only* has no dividing pillar but retains curved frames.
Roofs	Hipped, slate. Some gabled examples on S&D. Metal ventilators fitted.
Height of Operating Floor Above Rail Level	8 feet.
Stairs	External, with wooden steps and handrails and full-width landing at top. Porch around door.
Chimneys	Stove-pipe.
Special Features	Wooden supports for handrail of signalman's landing. In form of an 'X'.

* A few type '4' boxes were constructed of wood or stone. Where these materials were used , they were employed up to eaves level, and the arched lower windows were replaced with square frames.

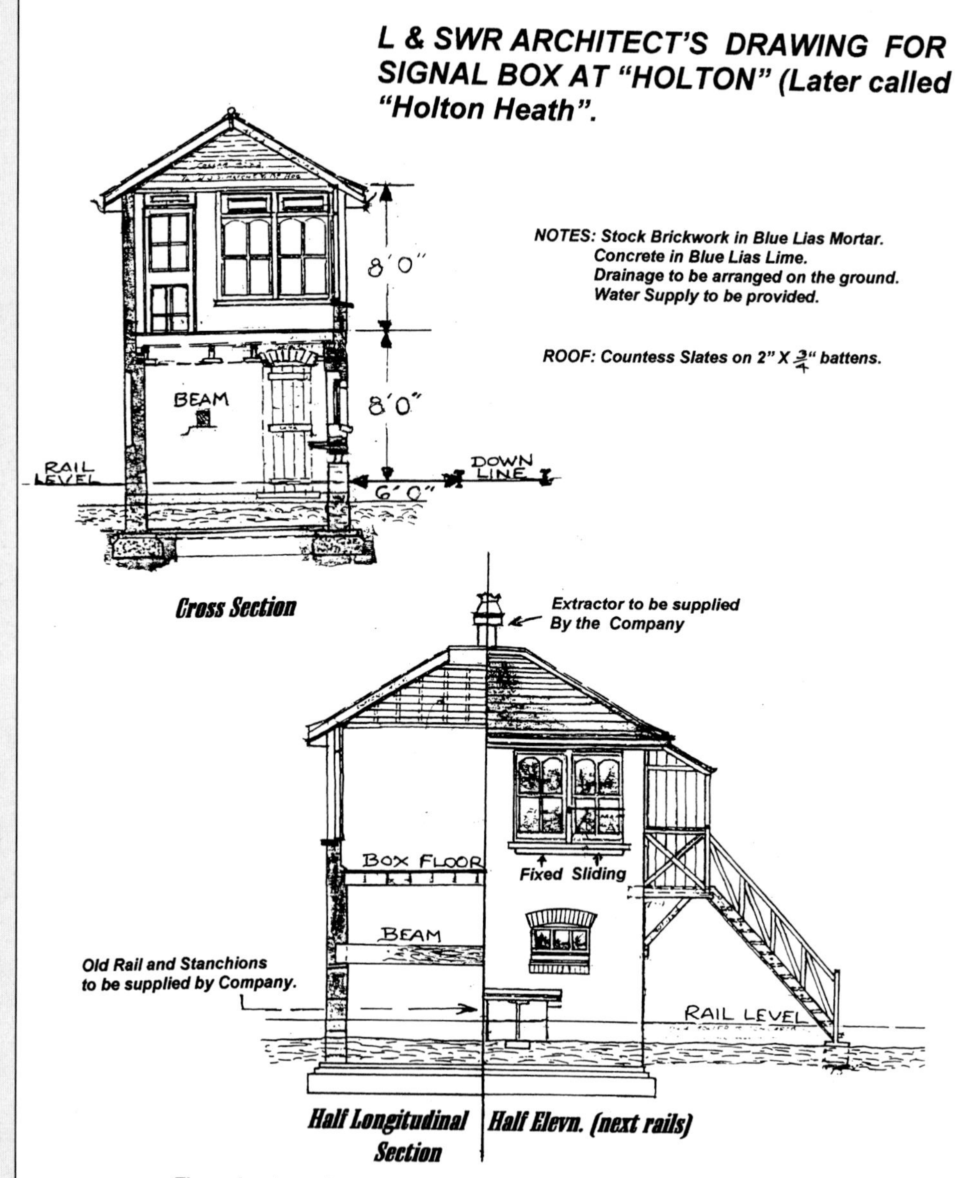

These drawings show a typical TYPE FOUR signal box, and were dated 24/03/1915. The box contained a 16-lever frame, and opened on 10-05-1915. The builder was a Mr. Bishop, probably a local tradesman.

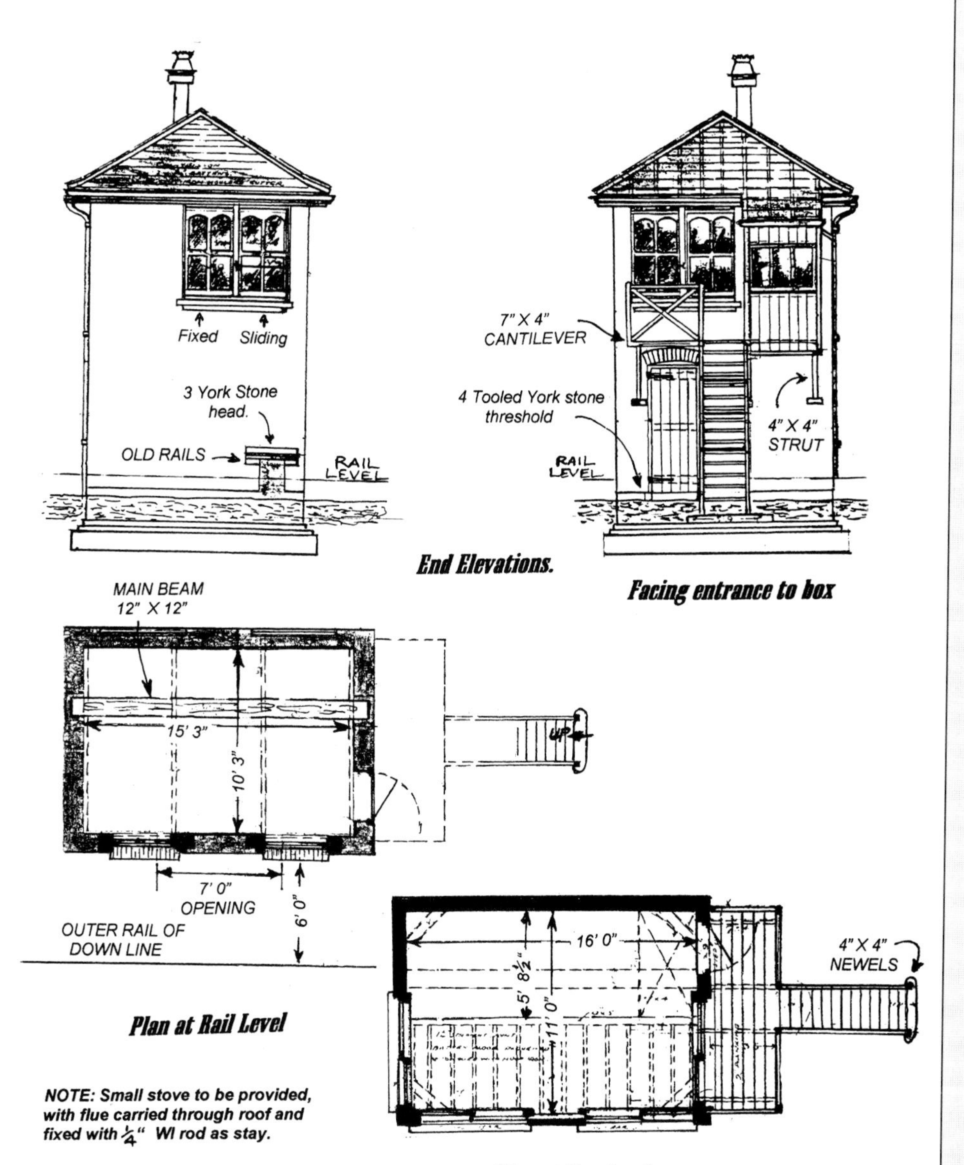

End Elevations.

Facing entrance to box

Plan at Rail Level

Plan at Box Level

NOTE: Small stove to be provided, with flue carried through roof and fixed with ¼" WI rod as stay.

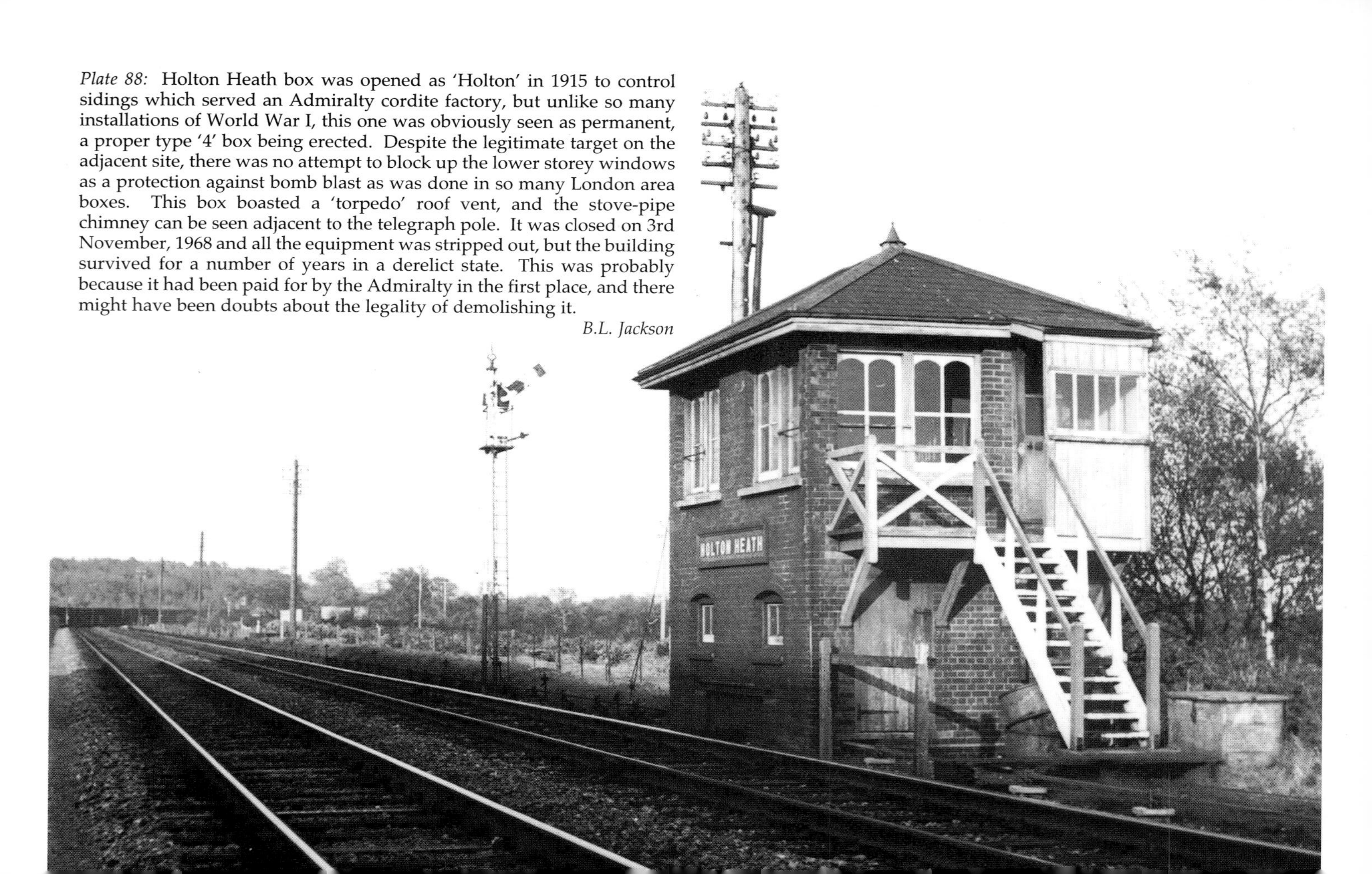

Plate 88: Holton Heath box was opened as 'Holton' in 1915 to control sidings which served an Admiralty cordite factory, but unlike so many installations of World War I, this one was obviously seen as permanent, a proper type '4' box being erected. Despite the legitimate target on the adjacent site, there was no attempt to block up the lower storey windows as a protection against bomb blast as was done in so many London area boxes. This box boasted a 'torpedo' roof vent, and the stove-pipe chimney can be seen adjacent to the telegraph pole. It was closed on 3rd November, 1968 and all the equipment was stripped out, but the building survived for a number of years in a derelict state. This was probably because it had been paid for by the Admiralty in the first place, and there might have been doubts about the legality of demolishing it.

B.L. Jackson

Plate 89: In the late 1890s the company was busy shortening the sections between Winchester, Micheldever, and Basingstoke. Many boxes provided in connection with this work were ground-level and little more than huts, but Roundwood was a full-size type '4'. The actual opening date is uncertain, but the style of box is certainly consistent with it being part of this programme. It was opened as 'Litchfield', but in 1953 it was given the name 'Roundwood' to avoid confusion with Litchfield on the neighbouring Didcot, Newbury, and Southampton line. Like most of the boxes on this section of the main line which crosses the chalk downs of central Hampshire, it was in a lonely spot and very difficult of access, so photographs are rare. It worked running signals only, so the frame contained only about six levers. Latterly it came to life on Summer Saturdays only, when a relief signalman had to make his way there from Winchester or Basingstoke, but it was taken out of commission on 25th July, 1966. *Oakwood Press Collection*

Plate 90: Fairfax Road (Teddington) was opened on 24th September, 1916, and because of its location close to London the locking room windows have been bricked up. In this case the wooden lean-to porch had windows in it, but these were not always provided. The usual neat appearance of a type '4' was somewhat marred by the crooked stove-pipe chimney! The box contained a 10-lever frame and gate wheel, and closed on 30th April, 1973 when the adjacent level crossing was also abolished.

John Scrace

Plate 91: St Denys was a type '4' with a few interesting differences. It had been opened in 1897 as 'Dukes Road Crossing', and the corner of the box nearest to the camera was splayed to accommodate the angle of the gates on the skew level crossing. The roof line is also unusual because, when built, the box was attached to a house. The crossing was replaced by an overbridge when quadrupling was carried out to Northam Junction in 1902. This box had 55 levers to which 2 were added by 1945. It was closed on 11th October, 1981 when the area was taken over by Eastleigh Panel. *J.P. Morris*

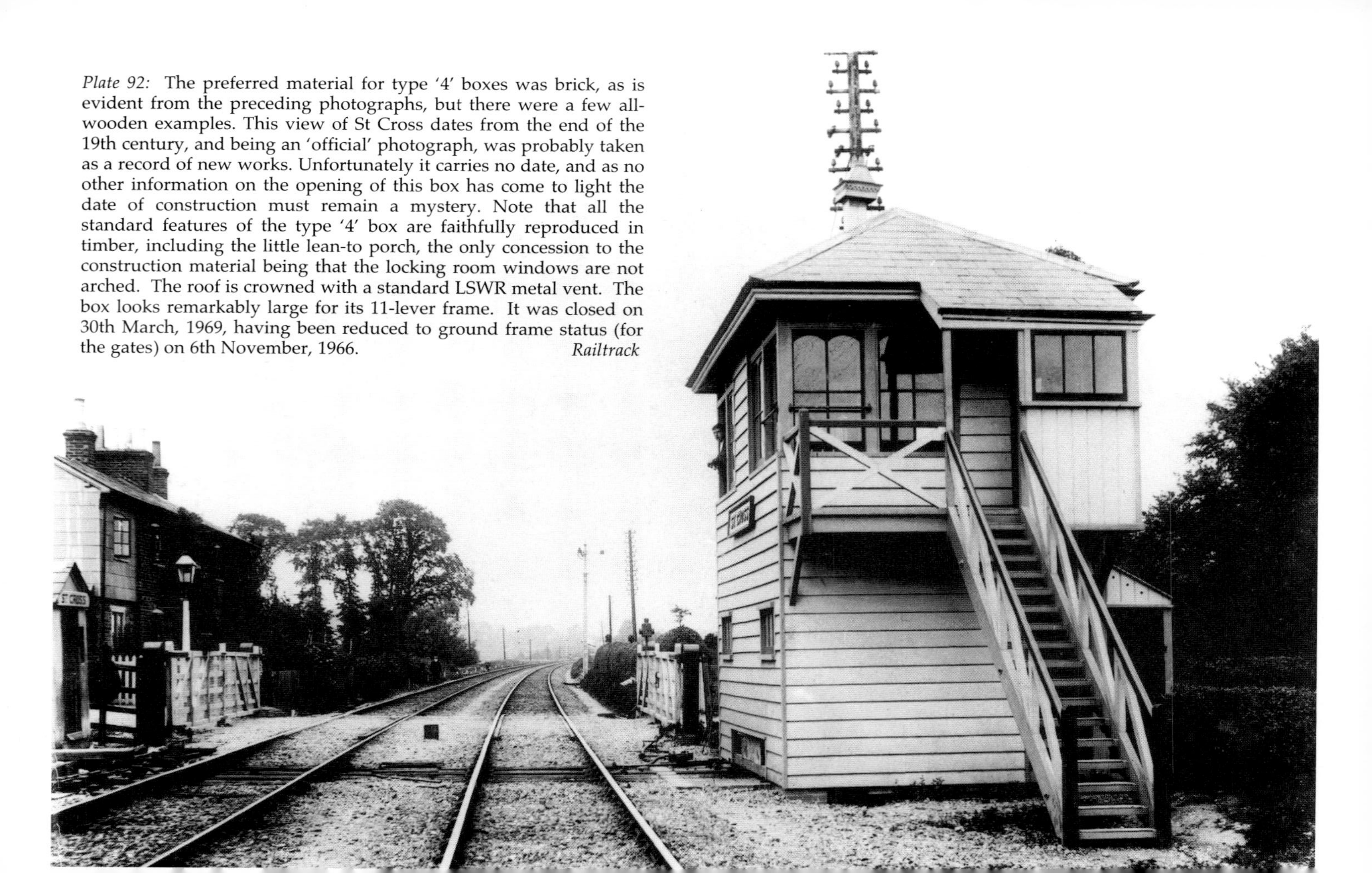

Plate 92: The preferred material for type '4' boxes was brick, as is evident from the preceding photographs, but there were a few all-wooden examples. This view of St Cross dates from the end of the 19th century, and being an 'official' photograph, was probably taken as a record of new works. Unfortunately it carries no date, and as no other information on the opening of this box has come to light the date of construction must remain a mystery. Note that all the standard features of the type '4' box are faithfully reproduced in timber, including the little lean-to porch, the only concession to the construction material being that the locking room windows are not arched. The roof is crowned with a standard LSWR metal vent. The box looks remarkably large for its 11-lever frame. It was closed on 30th March, 1969, having been reduced to ground frame status (for the gates) on 6th November, 1966. *Railtrack*

Plate 93: Wadebridge station was remodelled in 1899 and received a new signal box at each end. This lovely view, although taken in BR days, is full of LSWR atmosphere, complete with veteran 'T9' locomotive. Here stone was used in the construction of the type '4' box instead of the usual brick, but otherwise it is quite a standard building. The single storey lean-to section with the two doors facing the camera contained a toilet and a store. One of the locking room windows has been blocked up. The reason is obscure, but this seems to have been done at quite a number of boxes. Originally the box had 31 levers, but 12 more were added in 1907, apparently without enlarging the box! It was closed on 17th December, 1967 when, with only a little freight traffic remaining, all points in the station area were converted to hand operation.

Alan Postlethwaite

Plate 94: Another stone type '4' box was opened at Padstow in 1899, and here again one of the locking room windows was subsequently blanked off. The signalman here could claim to be the most distant from the company's headquarters at Waterloo - 259 miles! The box contained an 18-lever Stevens' frame, and was closed on 9th January, 1966.

C.L. Caddy Collection

Plate 95: At first glance this box at Virginia Water ('A' box until 26th June, 1966) would seem to be a standard type '4', but in fact there were windows in both sides of the building which made it a '4A'. It stood on the island platform with the Reading line on one side (from which the picture is taken) and the Weybridge line on the other, so the signalman required an equal outlook each way. The design was so symmetrical that it was impossible to differentiate between the back and front of the box, as they looked exactly alike. It dated from 1898 and contained a 39-lever frame supplied by Messrs Evans, O'Donnell to the Stevens' pattern. Originally there were three locking room windows on each side, blocked up in later years. A toilet for the signalman's use was added in an extension to the porch, but there were few other alterations. Note the standard LSWR-pattern roof vent. This box closed on 8th September, 1974. *John Scrace*

Plate 96: Yeovil Junction 'A' replaced an older box when the layout was enlarged in 1909, and was also a '4A' with windows on both sides. It has had an interesting history. Initially the frame, of Stevens' pattern, was of 60 levers, but as part of the scheme for singling the Salisbury-Exeter line the box ceased to control the main line on 7th May, 1967 and most of the levers became spare. At that point it was not possible to cross two trains at this important station, the single line section extending from Sherborne to Chard Junction, but experience quickly demonstrated the inadequacy of this arrangement and it was decided the reinstate the double line from Sherborne. However, the Western Region (who now controlled the area) did not seem very conversant with Stevens' locking, so rather than interfere unduly with the old frame they ripped it out and replaced it with a 45-lever frame of GWR vertical tappet type. At the same time all the windows were replaced with standard WR (ex-GWR) frames, which has somewhat altered the appearance of the box. This is one of the few boxes featured in this book to remain in use at the time of writing, even though it does now have a distinctly Great Western look! *B.L. Jackson*

Plate 97

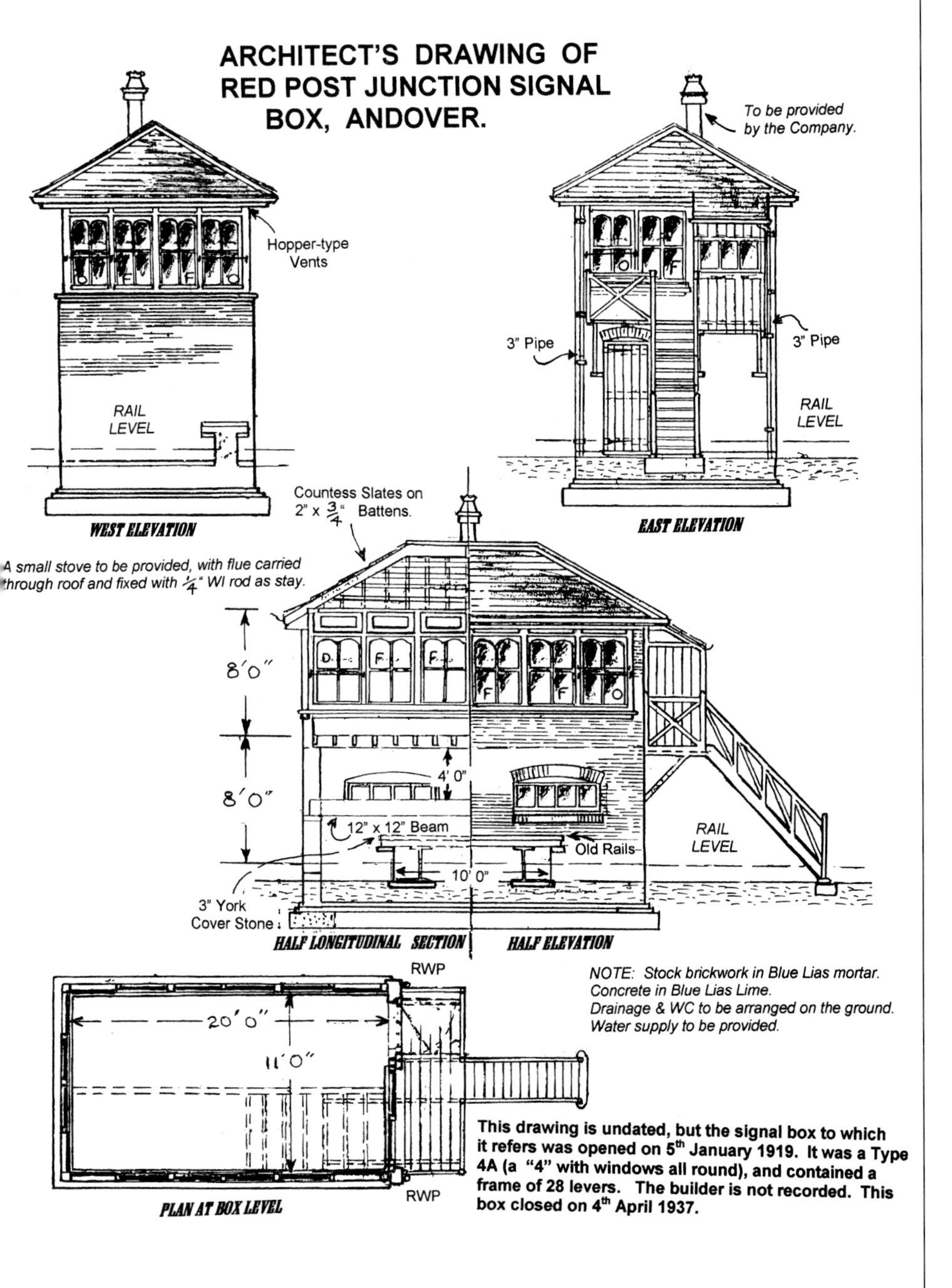

This drawing is undated, but the signal box to which it refers was opened on 5th January 1919. It was a Type 4A (a "4" with windows all round), and contained a frame of 28 levers. The builder is not recorded. This box closed on 4th April 1937.

Plate 98: The age of power signalling arrived early on the LSWR, an experimental installation of low-pressure pneumatic equipment being installed at Grateley in July 1901, complete with some automatic signals between there and Andover Junction. See architectural plan *Plates 99 & 100*. *B.L. Jackson*

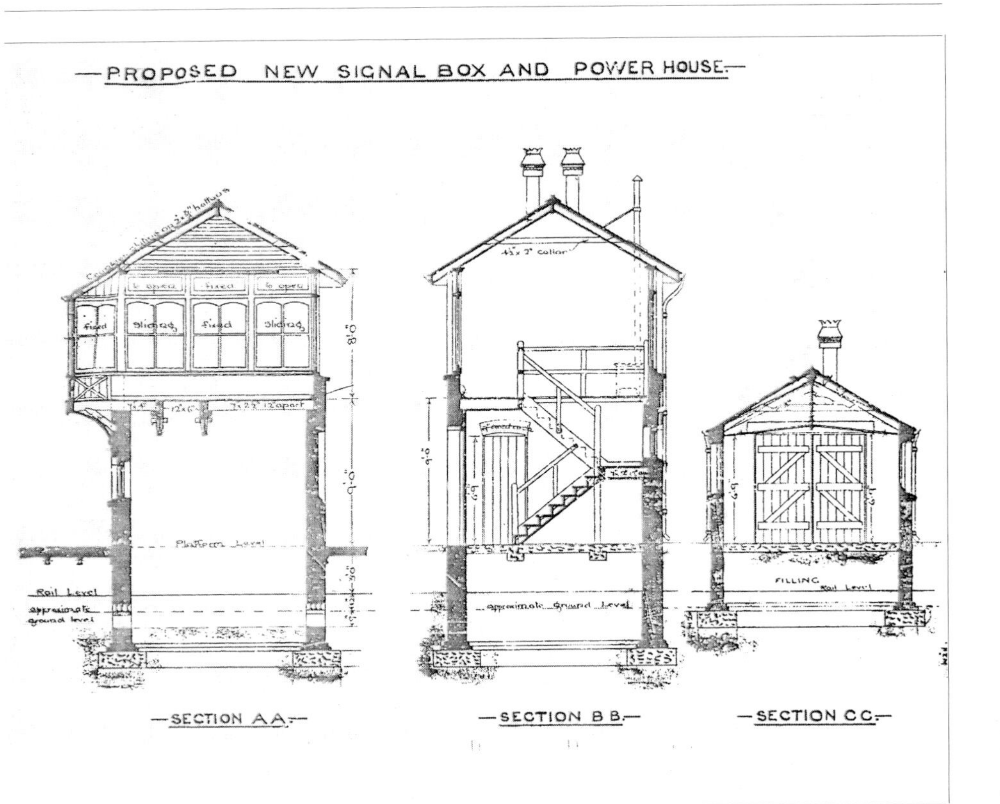

Plates 99 & 100: To house the frame of 70 slides this large type '4A' box was constructed at Grateley. In many ways it was a standard structure of the larger sort, with a small window in the middle of the central brick pillar, one oddity being the bay window at the far end of the building. This was provided in this instance because of the length of the new layout, and as track circuits at the time solely acted as a means of controlling the auto signals and were not indicated in the box, the signalman needed a 'look out' from which to observe the farthest sets of points during shunting. As shown in the architectural plan, a power house for the supply of compressed air was originally attached to the building, but when the pneumatic frame was replaced by a conventional mechanical one in 1921 this was demolished and a standard wooden exterior staircase provided on its site. A mechanical frame of 66 levers was longer than the power frame of 70 slides, so the space occupied by the original internal staircase was used up. The wooden door in the front wall was the signalman's old entrance. Grateley box was closed on 2nd May, 1968.

Railtrack

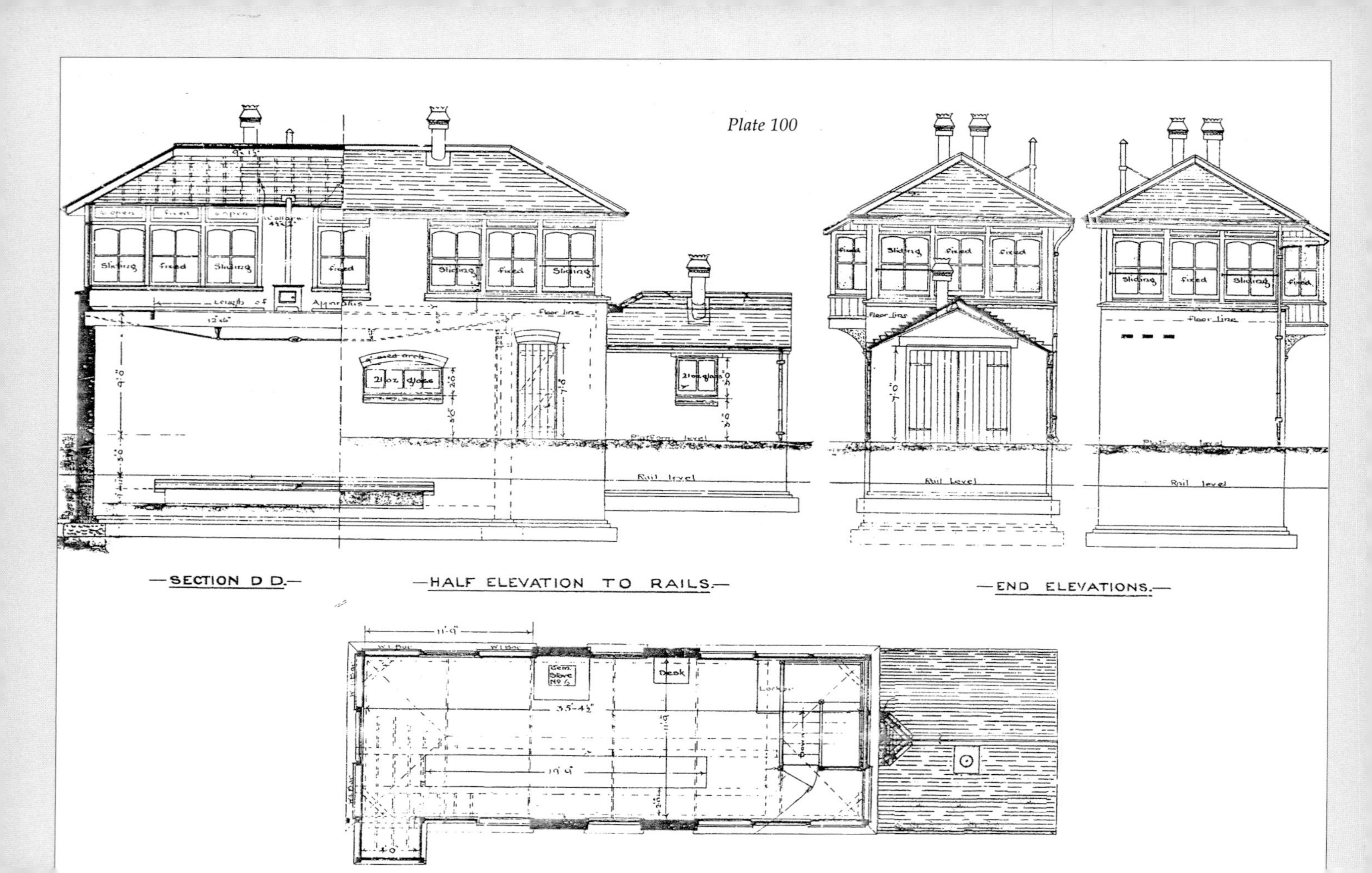
Plate 100
SECTION D D.
HALF ELEVATION TO RAILS.
END ELEVATIONS.
Sliding
fixed
floor line
Platform level
Rail level
21 oz glass
Cem. Stove No 5
Desk
Locker
Down
3.5'-4½"
19' 9"
11' 9"
W.I. Box

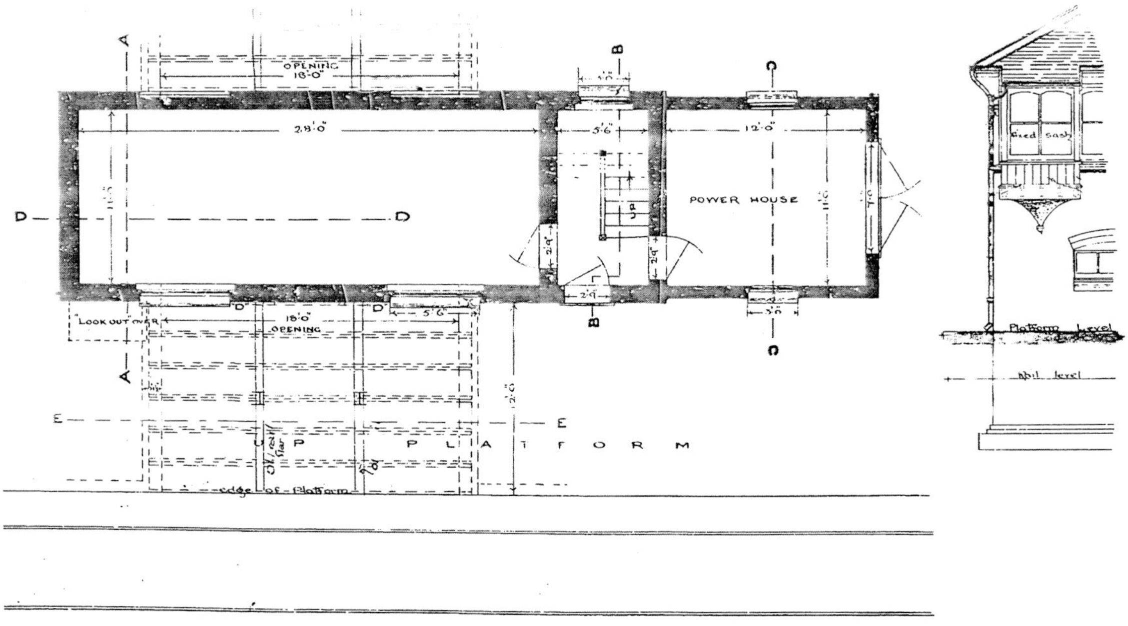
OPENING 18'-0"
28'-0"
5'-6"
12'-0"
POWER HOUSE
UP
"LOOK OUT" OVER
18'-0" OPENING
5'-6"
UP PLATFORM
edge of Platform
Fixed Sash
Platform Level
Rail level

—PLAN AT PLATFORM LEVEL.—

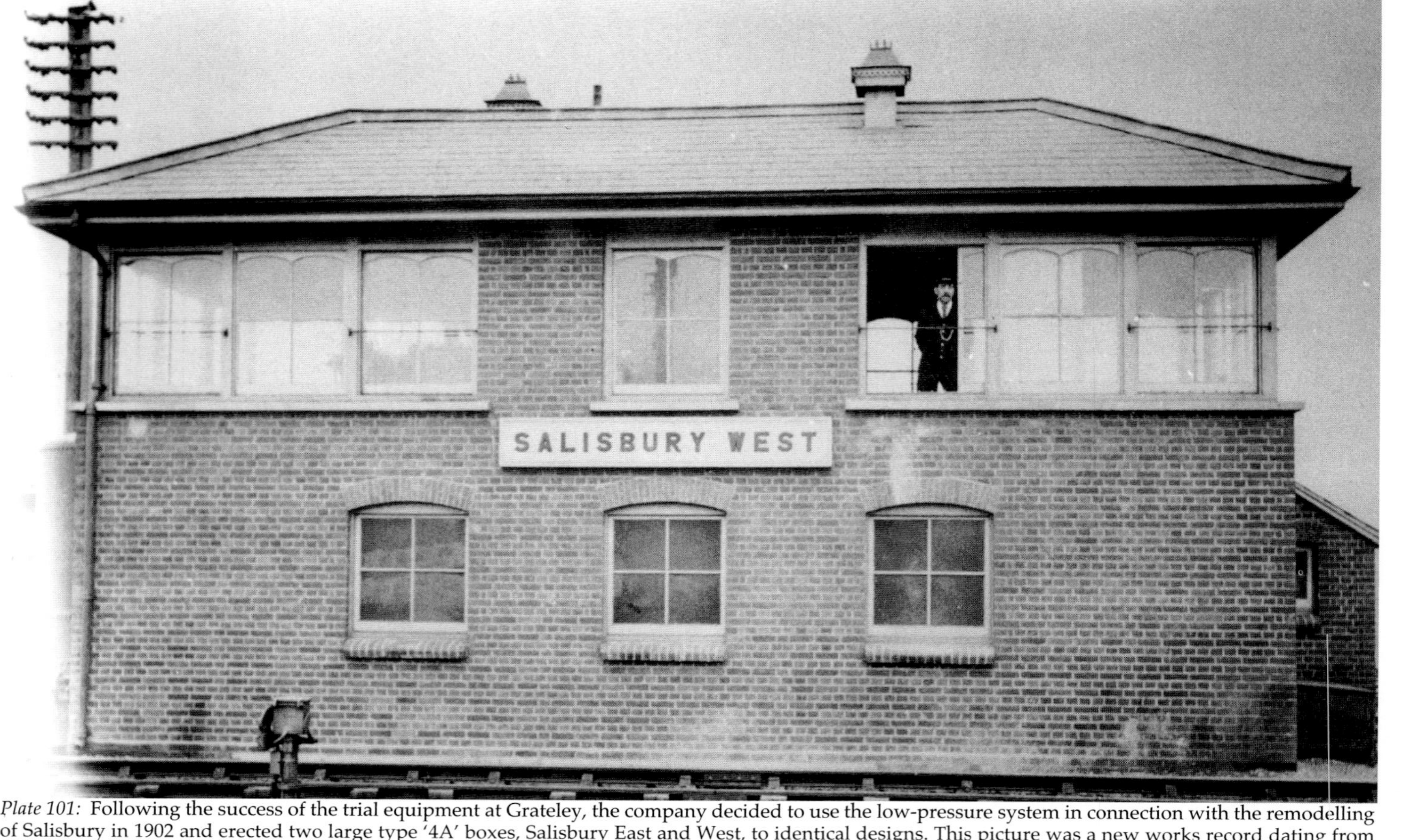

Plate 101: Following the success of the trial equipment at Grateley, the company decided to use the low-pressure system in connection with the remodelling of Salisbury in 1902 and erected two large type '4A' boxes, Salisbury East and West, to identical designs. This picture was a new works record dating from shortly after the boxes were opened, and shows Salisbury West in original condition, complete with two standard LSWR roof vents. As at Grateley, the stairs were internal, and a window pierced the central brick pillar.

Railtrack

Plate 102: The interior of Salisbury West box as first opened, with the mechanical locking between the 64 slides exposed to view. Later this was enclosed with polished wooden panelling, and looked much tidier (compare with *Plate 106*). *Railtrack*

Plate 103: During World War II both the Salisbury boxes were given flat concrete roofs which made them look rather more modern than they actually were, and the locking room windows were bricked up. This was how they remained until closure on 21st August, 1981. The compressed air reservoir tank can be clearly seen at the end of the building farthest from the photographer.

Railtrack

Plate 104: Some of the low-pressure automatic signals associated with the Woking-Basingstoke scheme. Engineering drawings of the original signals for the experimental installation at Grateley in 1901 show them to be almost identical, although that section being only double track, they were not mounted on bridges. They enjoyed a long working life, not being replaced by colour-lights until the mid-1960s. *Railtrack*

Plate 105: The LSWR was quite content to continue the use of type '4' boxes for power signalling schemes instead of developing something new, and the pneumatic boxes on the section of main line between Woking and Basingstoke (1903-1906) were all of this design. Externally this box at Brookwood looked exactly like a conventional mechanical box, but inside was a low-pressure frame of 40 'slides'. Some of these power boxes were given internal staircases, but in this case an external flight with a porch was provided in truly traditional style. *B.L. Jackson Collection*

Plate 106: The pristine interior of Brookwood in 1962, showing the panelling which latterly enclosed the mechanical locking between the slides (compare with *Plate 102*). Track Circuit Block applied on the main lines, but the three-position instrument in the foreground controlled the line from Ash Vale. The large oil lamp was for emergency use in the event of a power cut. Brookwood box closed on 5th June, 1966. *Railtrack*

Plate 107: As mentioned in the text, some standard type '4' boxes appeared on lines that were not owned by the LSWR. Tidworth was a MSWJR example, which became GWR property at the Grouping. It even sported an LSWR roof vent! The precise opening date is uncertain, as the line was opened for military manoeuvres traffic only in 1901, public passenger traffic not commencing until July the following year. The closure date is equally uncertain, the line being taken over by the War Department in November 1955, but it is thought to have been abolished soon after. It contained a frame of 26 levers.
B.L. Jackson

Plate 108: Another MSWJR type '4' was Swindon Town 'A', which contained a frame of 17 levers and was opened in 1881 but rebuilt in the new approved style in 1904. The brick chimney stack, not a regular type '4' feature, would appear to be left over from the original structure. The 'B' box at this station was rebuilt in the unusual form of an all-timber '4B' (no central pillar). Passenger services were withdrawn on 11th September, 1961, but for a while there were enough freight movements to justify retention of the signal boxes. They were eventually abolished on 9th March, 1964. *C.L. Caddy*

Plate 109: The Somerset & Dorset Joint Line also had some signal boxes of fairly standard type '4' pattern, although often they exhibited differences of detail. This box at Stalbridge had replaced an old structure in 1903, and as the LSWR held responsibility for signalling matters on this line it was not surprising that their latest design was used. The only differences between this building and one on the company's system proper are the absence of a full-width landing and details of the porch. Generally the latter were of the lean-to type and were devoid of decoration, but here it has a flat roof with ornamental moulding around the top. Stalbridge had an 18-lever frame and gate wheel, and it closed with the passing of the S&D on 7th March, 1966.

Oakwood Press Collection

Plate 110: Glastonbury was resignalled and received a new box in 1901. It was an all-timber type '4', but different from the standard type in having full-width side windows. The frame consisted of 28 levers, including quite a number of push-and-pulls. This box also lasted until the closure of the line on 7th March, 1966.

Photomatic

Plate 111: Feltham Junction Box dated from October 1921 when the new marshalling yard was being laid out, and contained a 61-lever frame of Stevens' pattern, although at that late date it would have been supplied by another manufacturer. By that time the company had standardised on 'back-to-traffic' frames, which made it practicable to dispense with the central brick pillar of the original type '4s' and have a continuous run of windows along the front, this style being categorised as '4B'. Apart from this, the curved-top windows, hipped roof, metal ventilators, and stove-pipe chimney were standard type '4' details. The marshalling yard was taken out of use on 2nd March, 1969, so from then until the box closed on 8th September, 1974 the frame contained a large number of spare levers.
Author's Collection

Plate 112: The interior of the busy Feltham Junction box, with the signalman setting up the route into the marshalling yard. *Author's Collection*

Plate 113: Moorewood Sidings was the newest box on the S&D line, not being opened until 1914. It was an early example of a 'back to traffic' lever frame, which contained 19 levers. Although it had many type '4' features the gable roof was unusual, as was the rather high opening for the lead-off bed. This box was abolished on 5th July, 1965.

C.L. Caddy

Plate 114: As mentioned in the text, designs distinctly similar to the LSWR type '4' were perpetuated by the newly-formed Southern Railway for some years after 1923. This 90-lever box, Exeter Central 'A', was opened on 15th June, 1927 - more than four years after the Grouping - yet at first glance it appeared to be a perfectly standard '4A'. However, closer inspection shows the detail differences wrought by the new management to make this structure actually a type '11A'. Note that the upper window frames are now straight instead of having the pleasantly curved tops of the type '4s', and that one slope of the hipped roof (not readily obvious in this photograph) is extended to form a porch over the full-width landing at the top of the signalman's steps, which are of prefabricated concrete instead of traditional wood. These were typical type '11' features, the basic model having no central brick pillar dividing the front windows. It is the presence of this latter feature which makes this example an '11A'. *B.L. Jackson*

Plate 115: Between Clapham Junction and Waterloo most of the line is on a viaduct which allowed little lineside space for conventional signal boxes. Boxes on this section were therefore built on bridges spanning the tracks, which not only overcame the siting problem but also afforded the signalman a view of his layout far superior to anything that could be obtained from an ordinary two-storey building. All these boxes were 'non-standard' and were treated as special cases. This picture of Waterloo 'A' shows the second box at this location, compare with *Plate 7*, and gives some idea of the complexities of semaphore signalling at a large terminal station. It was opened in 1872, and contained a Saxby 'rocker' frame of 109 levers. It was greatly enlarged in 1885, and again in 1911, but survived until 18th October, 1936 when the [illegible]

Chapter Six

Non-Standard Boxes (Post-1873)

As explained in Chapter One, all boxes erected prior to 1873 were individual projects and did not conform to any standard designs, but from that year until the end of the LSWR as an independent company a whole range of 'standards' was available. It is therefore very odd that boxes of non-standard, and sometimes quite strange, appearance continued to be built here and there for reasons which are now totally obscure.

One possible explanation could be that use was being made of surplus materials left over from other work. The company was very economically minded, and would not have considered throwing away window frames and other joinery intended for some other type of building simply because these bits and pieces were not designed for signal boxes. There is indeed a strong possibility that as the deadline for proper signalling imposed by the 1889 Parliamentary Act approached the company had to undertake a few rather hurried schemes, making use of whatever materials were to hand.

In other cases the site could have proved unstable. The intention might have been to erect, say, a standard type '3', but this might have been changed at the last minute if there was difficulty in obtaining sound foundations, the Engineer being left to put up a suitable building using any standard parts that were still suitable but virtually having to re-design the box.

Yet another contributory factor was the necessity to provide the signalman with an overall view of his layout, the track circuit remaining something of a rarity until the late 1920s. Where the layout was on a curve or was crossed by overbridges a 'special' box was sometimes required, either much taller or much lower than the standard, to give an adequate outlook. Many such boxes were in fact basically standard structures, but their extreme dimensions gave them a different appearance.

There were, however, a number of boxes which seem to have been deliberately built to non-standard designs, and no explanation for these is forthcoming. Some of these are illustrated in the pages that follow, but it has not been possible to include an example of every such building.

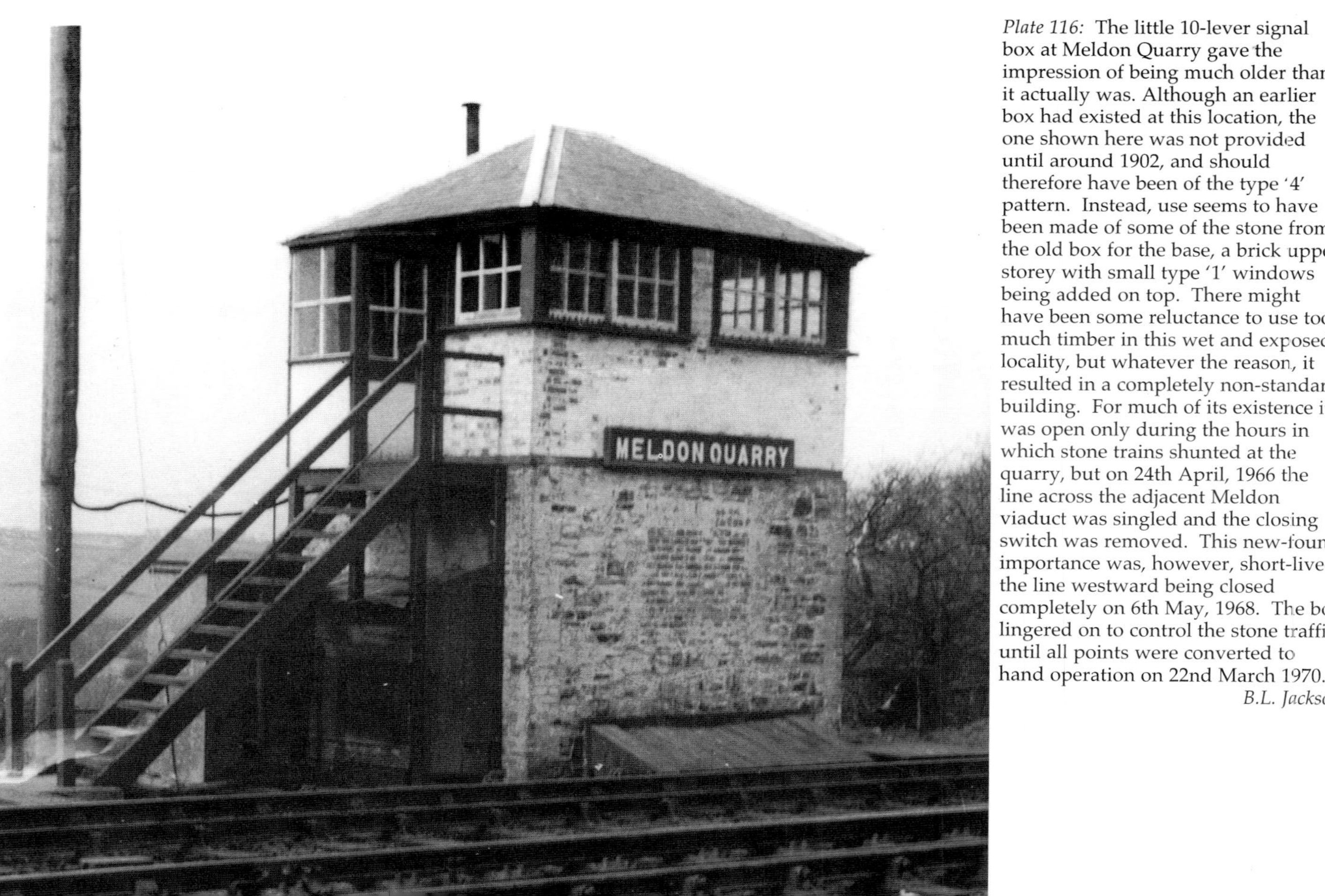

Plate 116: The little 10-lever signal box at Meldon Quarry gave the impression of being much older than it actually was. Although an earlier box had existed at this location, the one shown here was not provided until around 1902, and should therefore have been of the type '4' pattern. Instead, use seems to have been made of some of the stone from the old box for the base, a brick upper storey with small type '1' windows being added on top. There might have been some reluctance to use too much timber in this wet and exposed locality, but whatever the reason, it resulted in a completely non-standard building. For much of its existence it was open only during the hours in which stone trains shunted at the quarry, but on 24th April, 1966 the line across the adjacent Meldon viaduct was singled and the closing switch was removed. This new-found importance was, however, short-lived, the line westward being closed completely on 6th May, 1968. The box lingered on to control the stone traffic until all points were converted to hand operation on 22nd March 1970.

B.L. Jackson

Plate 117: Dorchester box dated from 1878, and was a most unusual structure, not least because the 25-lever frame was installed end-on to traffic! As can be seen from the photograph, the box was extremely lofty to allow the signalman a view over the roof of the neighbouring engine shed, the over-sailing operating floor giving further assistance in this respect. Close inspection reveals it as a heavily modified type '1', with standard windows and hipped slate roof, adapted to suit the rather peculiar nature of the site. In 1931 the frame was extended to 33 levers, apparently without having to make any extension to the building, and in this state it survived until replaced by a new box of BR design on 22nd February, 1959. *R.C. Riley*

Plate 118: Barnes Junction dated from the quadrupling of the line from Putney in 1885, and occupied an island site between the up and down lines. It therefore had windows all the way around, this view being of the back of the box! Much of the woodwork had a type '3' air, but the window frames were non-standard and the plain brick base (heavily patched in this 1950s picture) without recesses was more akin to a type '2'. *R.K. Blencowe*

Plate 119: The type '3' was really a brick and timber design, but this little box at Shawford Station, which dated from June 1882, seems to be an attempt at building one entirely from wood. Certainly the window frames with their toplights and the roof vent were standard type '3' features, but the main structure consisted of a wooden frame covered with vertical boarding instead of the usual recessed brickwork. When opened it contained 10 levers, although some shunt signals were added at a later date and the frame might have been slightly extended. The building was large enough to accommodate at least 16 levers, so minor alterations could have been done without lengthening the building. It was abolished on 15th March, 1931, the area being brought under the control of the enlarged Shawford Junction box.

R.K. Blencowe Collection

Plate 120: Cosham Junction was an amalgam of styles. The window frames were narrow type '3B' sliding sashes, but other features such as the roof vent, railed walkway, vertical boarding beneath the windows, and recessed brick base were definitely type '3'! An oddity was that toplight windows were only applied in the ends, the front having a narrow band of vertical boarding above the main windows. Whilst this could have been a later modification, the woodwork appears to be all of a similar age. The two locking room windows had been bricked in, probably a wartime measure in view of the vulnerability of the Portsmouth area. On 5th May, 1968 the Cosham triangle came under the control of a new panel at Portsmouth, this 14-lever box then being abolished. *John Scrace*

Plate 121: Fareham East dated from 1903, when the layout was being considerably enlarged to accommodate Meon Valley trains and also in connection with the deviation line (avoiding the Fareham tunnels) which was opened the following year. Like many of the larger structures it 'did its own thing' rather than follow strictly standard designs. The recessed brick base was suggestive of the type '3s', but the windows lacked toplights and were more like those used in '3Bs'. It is not known whether this box ever boasted a roof vent, but it would have been most unusual for a building of that size to have been without. Following the closure of the West box on 5th December, 1971 it became simply 'Fareham', but its layout remained largely intact until after closure of the deviation line in 1973 when the trackwork was simplified and the frame shortened to 40 levers. Closure came on 20th June, 1982, when the area was brought under the control of Eastleigh panel box.

John Scrace

Plate 122: Kingston Junction looked more like an LBSCR box than anything erected by the LSWR, and might actually have been a Saxby & Farmer building. The diagonal boarding was a novel feature! It is thought to have been installed in 1900 , about the time when signalling on the 'South Western' reached its peak with every possible movement provided for, which resulted in a frame of 70 levers. The station was rebuilt in 1935 and the low-level terminal platforms abolished, which greatly simplified the track layout and gave rise to a lot of spare levers. Subsequently the frame was shortened to 40 levers, but the box remained in use until 10th November, 1974.

John Scrace

Plate 123: Ascot West would seem to date from 1878, when a siding and crossover were installed there to serve a brickworks. This was just on the change-over point between type '2' and type '3' boxes, which may account for the somewhat different appearance of this box. The window frames were basically type '2', but there was no ornamental valence and the end windows ran the whole width of the building. This, plus some additional height, gave it a rather flimsy aspect. Another unusual feature was the very high lead-off opening, largely blocked off with panels. This box, which had a 16-lever Stevens' frame, was usually opened only to shunt the pick-up freights, although it enjoyed longer hours of use during the famous Ascot Races when the adjoining passenger platforms were pressed into service. It was taken out of use on 5th October, 1969 following a long period of closure. *John Scrace*

Plate 124: Portcreek Junction is recorded as being opened in January 1860, and must have contained one of the earliest interlocked lever frames. However, it was totally rebuilt in 1910, and this picture shows the all-timber structure that resulted. The box contained a 17-lever frame, and was very busy! Bursledon (*see next plate*) was opened the following year and was a very similar structure, but no others of the type are known. Portcreek closed on 5th May 1968, the area then being controlled from Portsmouth Panel. *John Scrace*

Plate 125: In March 1911 the section between Swanwick and Netley was doubled, a signal box being provided at Bursledon station. This was an all-timber building of horizontal boarding with a hipped slate roof and 'torpedo' vent, distinctly similar to Portcreek Junction which had been rebuilt the previous year. It contained a Saxby & Farmer frame of 18 levers and Sykes' Lock & Block instruments. This box was closed on 27th June, 1971.
B.L. Jackson

Plate 126

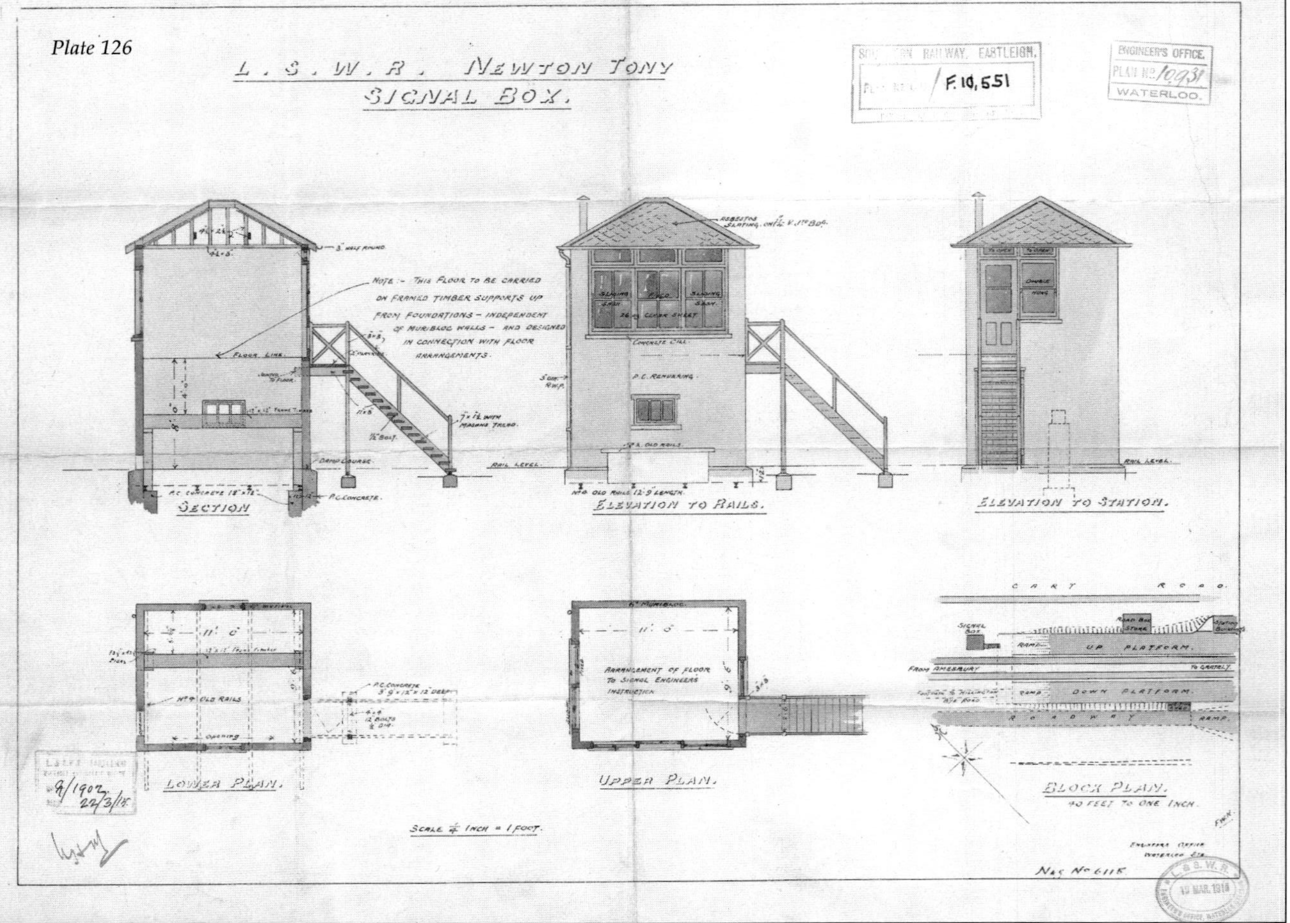

L. S. W. R. NEWTON TONY
SIGNAL BOX.

SOUTHERN RAILWAY, EARTLEIGH. F. 10,551

ENGINEER'S OFFICE. PLAN No. 10931 WATERLOO.

NOTE:- THIS FLOOR TO BE CARRIED ON FRAMED TIMBER SUPPORTS UP FROM FOUNDATIONS - INDEPENDENT OF MURIBLOC WALLS - AND DESIGNED IN CONNECTION WITH FLOOR ARRANGEMENTS.

FLOOR LINE.

DAMP COURSE.

RAIL LEVEL.

P.C. CONCRETE 18" x 12".

P.C. CONCRETE.

SECTION

ASBESTOS SLATING, ON 1¼" V. 1ST BDS.

SLIDING SASH. FIXED. SLIDING SASH. 26 oz CLEAR SHEET

CONCRETE CILL.

P.C. RENDERING.

No. 6 OLD RAILS 12' 9" LENGTH.

ELEVATION TO RAILS.

DOUBLE HUNG

RAIL LEVEL.

ELEVATION TO STATION.

11' 0"

No. 4 OLD RAILS

LOWER PLAN.

6" MURIBLOC.

11' 0"

ARRANGEMENT OF FLOOR TO SIGNAL ENGINEERS INSTRUCTION.

UPPER PLAN.

SCALE ¼ INCH = 1 FOOT.

C A R T R O A D.

SIGNAL BOX

UP PLATFORM.

FROM AMESBURY

TO GRATELY

DOWN PLATFORM.

R O A D W A Y

RAMP.

BLOCK PLAN.
40 FEET TO ONE INCH.

ENGINEERS OFFICE WATERLOO STN.

N & S No. 6115

9/1902. 22/3/15.

L. & S. W. R. 19 MAR 1918

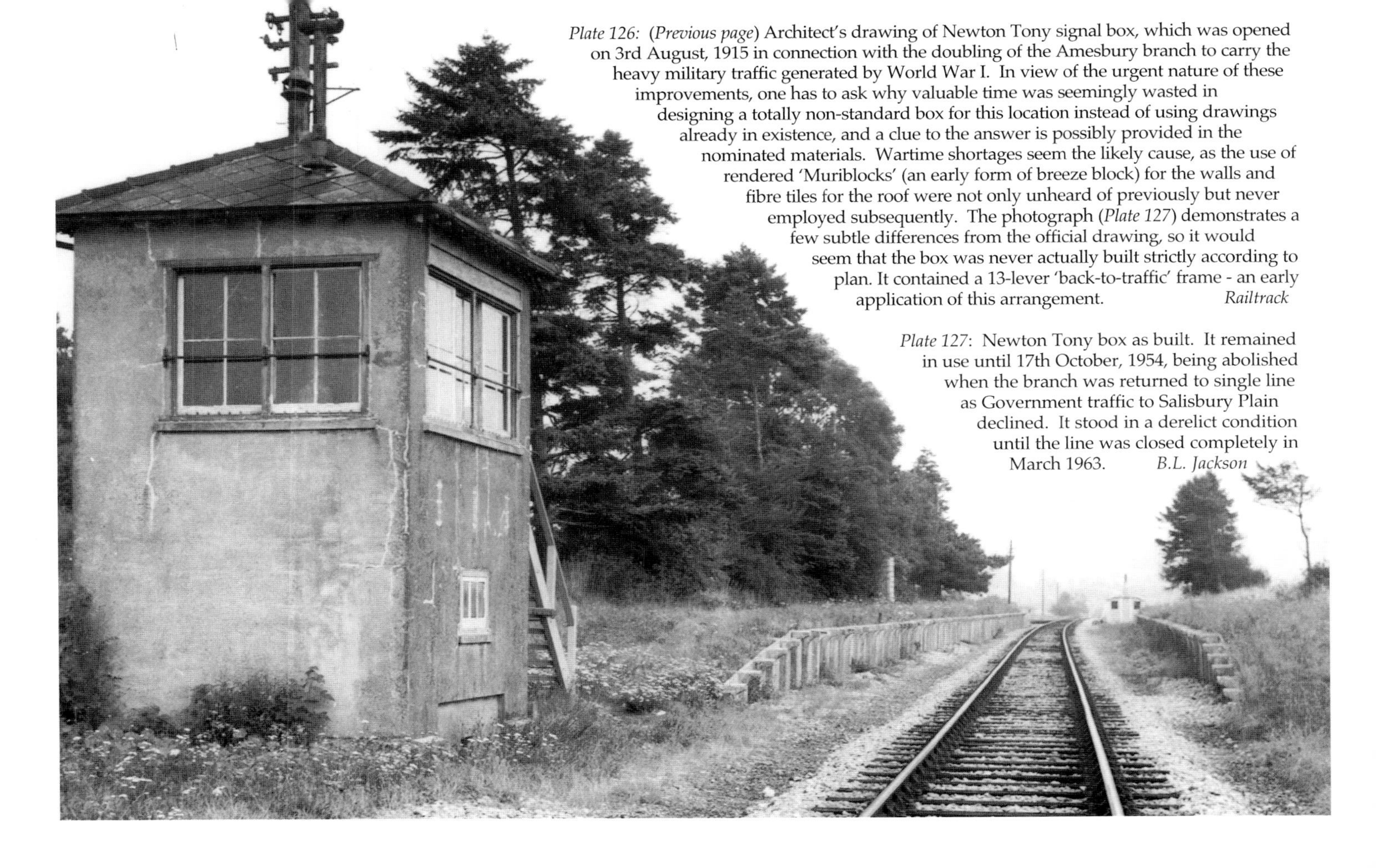

Plate 126: (*Previous page*) Architect's drawing of Newton Tony signal box, which was opened on 3rd August, 1915 in connection with the doubling of the Amesbury branch to carry the heavy military traffic generated by World War I. In view of the urgent nature of these improvements, one has to ask why valuable time was seemingly wasted in designing a totally non-standard box for this location instead of using drawings already in existence, and a clue to the answer is possibly provided in the nominated materials. Wartime shortages seem the likely cause, as the use of rendered 'Muriblocks' (an early form of breeze block) for the walls and fibre tiles for the roof were not only unheard of previously but never employed subsequently. The photograph (*Plate 127*) demonstrates a few subtle differences from the official drawing, so it would seem that the box was never actually built strictly according to plan. It contained a 13-lever 'back-to-traffic' frame - an early application of this arrangement. *Railtrack*

Plate 127: Newton Tony box as built. It remained in use until 17th October, 1954, being abolished when the branch was returned to single line as Government traffic to Salisbury Plain declined. It stood in a derelict condition until the line was closed completely in March 1963. *B.L. Jackson*

Plate 128: Some non-standard signal boxes were quite pleasing buildings, but Gunnersbury had nothing attractive about it whatsoever. Opened in 1893 as 'Gunnersbury East' in connection with layout improvements at the station, it had a plain brick base and wooden upper storey. The top-light windows seemed rather over-sized! Instead of windows lighting the locking room there were a pair of heavy wooden doors which gave the maintenance men good access to the mechanical connections. The general appearance was not enhanced by the toilet extension at the top of the stairs, the angle of the sloping roof having an unfortunate visual affect. Perhaps the best feature was the standard L SWR roof ventilator! The layout was much simplified in May 1932 and the West box was abolished, but this one lasted until 28th March, 1980 when Richmond box assumed control of the area.

John Scrace

Chapter Seven

Ground-Level Boxes

So far this book has concentrated mainly on 'elevated' signal boxes, in which the operating floor is raised above the locking. There was, however, a significant number of ground-level boxes which, being single-storey, required the use of specially designed lever frames with the locking encased above floor level. Known to generations of signalmen as 'knee frames' (because the levers were short and the locking case came up to about knee height) they were unpopular with the staff unless the layout contained no heavy pulls. The shortness of the levers prevented the signalman from obtaining a really good 'swing' without standing on the locking case and launching himself off it whilst grasping the lever, an exercise attended by considerable risk of personal injury in the event of a signal wire snapping! Partly for this reason, but also because the view obtainable from a ground-level box was very limited, they tended to be provided only at places with very small and simple layouts. They were ideal for level crossings, especially those with hand-operated gates where they spared the signalman countless trips up and down the stairs, and for intermediate block posts which operated nothing but running signals, but quite a number also appeared on branch lines constructed on a shoe-string in the 1890s and early part of the 20th century. There was also a tendency to use boxes of this type for the control of military sidings and other connections seen as 'temporary' installations during World War I.

Many ground-level boxes were of early date, some almost certainly being Block Huts erected in the 1860s during the spread of block working. In their original form these might have contained no levers, the policeman exhibiting appropriate hand signals to passing trains in association with the Block messages, the frames (always small) being a later refinement. Whilst the use of huts in connection with this work has been dealt with in Chapter One, and it is obvious that most of them were of a temporary nature pending the installation of locking frames, there must have been quite a few locations where the sections between stations were seen as too long for the smooth operation of traffic and where it was going to be necessary to maintain block posts even after the completion of the signalling programme, and the 'huts' at these locations would have been of more durable quality. Like other boxes of the period these did not follow any standard designs, but later two distinct types of ground-level box emerged, the types '5' and '6'.

The type '5' seems to have originated in 1892, when several boxes of that type were opened at crossings between Salisbury and Exeter. The structures were wholly of timber on a dwarf brick wall, the wooden framework being covered with horizontal boards, and the gable roofs were slated. The sliding windows were large in relation to the building, being three panes deep by two or three across. Some had brick chimney stacks, but others had stove-pipes. A small lean-to porch protected the doorway. The only ornamentation on these boxes were spike finials at each end of the roof ridge, and they were otherwise

Plate 129: The opening date of this miniature brick signal box at Honiton Incline is not recorded, but it probably came into use with the doubling of the line in 1869/70. The block section from Colyton Junction (later 'Seaton Junction') to Honiton was a lengthy one, and included a long, steep incline and a tunnel, exactly the sort of place which saw the introduction of Block Working ahead of the main programme. This view, taken in 1932 with signalman Harry Osmond, shows the box in its original condition. Later the walls were rendered with cement and painted cream! Train crews knew it as 'Hut Box', the building being so low on the ground that a man standing at the lever frame inside had his head just level with the axle boxes of passing trains. Many boxes of this type doubtless existed in the early days, but they were replaced by something better as layouts and signalling developed. Honiton Incline never saw much development and the site was very inaccessible, so it remained virtually untouched until the run-down of traffic in Western Region days, not closing until 6th March, 1966. *Mike Clement Collection*

unadorned. No official drawings of type '5' boxes seem to have survived, and given their distinct similarity to structures found on other railways, a contractor's involvement seems likely. The design does not appear to have been used on the LSWR after 1900, when the company produced a design of its own, the type '6'.

The type '6' presented a lower, squatter, appearance. Hipped roofs were back in fashion, although the small size of some of these buildings made them almost come to a point, and metal roof vents were fitted as standard. There is no record of any type '6' box with a brick chimney, all of them having combustion stoves and the attendant stovepipe. Again the basic structure was entirely wood, the frame being covered by horizontal boards, but the windows were reduced to two panes in depth. Boxes of this type appeared on cheaply constructed or hurriedly resignalled branch lines, examples being found on the Amesbury branch, the Lyme Regis branch (properly signalled in 1906), and at Budleigh Salterton (1902).

Although the type '6' was definitely a ground-level design there was one elevated example, Amesbury Junction (1904), in which the standard type '6' top was simply erected on a tall wooden base.

Alongside these two standard designs and the multiplicity of individualistic structures stood a number of ground-level boxes adapted from ordinary 'elevated' designs. There were ground-level examples of types '1', '3', and '4' boxes, some of which involved the re-use of secondhand woodwork and window frames, but no type '2s' are thought to have been so adapted. No records have come to light concerning the signal box structures used in connection with World War I installations. In view of the short life of many of these, and the fact that it would probably have been unwise to be seen with a camera near military camps and depots, this is not surprising.

Summary of Boxes Classified as Type '5'

Period of Construction	1892 to 1900
Basic Structure	Timber framework covered with horizontal boarding, mounted on dwarf brick wall.
Windows	Large, sliding. Three panes deep by two or three across.
Roofs	Gable, slated, with wooden spike finials.
Height of Operating Floor	Ground level.
Chimneys	Some brick stacks, mostly stove-pipes.

Summary of Boxes Classified as Type '6'

Period of Construction	1900 to *c.*1915
Basic Structure	Timber framework covered with horizontal boarding.
Windows	Small, sliding. Two panes deep by two or three across.
Roofs	Hipped, slated, with metal vent.
Height of Operating Floor	Ground level. One elevated example at 8 ft.
Chimneys	Stove-pipes.

Plate 130: Another ground-level box from the 'block hut' era could be found at Steventon, a lonely spot on the main Southampton line. It stood about halfway between Micheldever station and the junction with the Exeter line at Battledown, so would have been a useful regulating point from the earliest days. The all-brick construction and slate roof with ornamental ridge tiles certainly suggest that it was considered a permanent structure rather than a temporary expedient for the introduction of the Block System, the company doubtless realising that the volume of traffic passing over this line would never allow Micheldever-Battledown to be worked as a single section. The porch may have been a later addition, as was the little lean-to 'privvy' in the background, but the building does not seem to have changed greatly throughout its life. It eventually closed on 19th July, 1966, when this section of line was converted to Track Circuit Block with automatic signals. *Oakwood Press Collection*

Plate 131: Standard type '5' ground-level box at Tisbury Gates, which was opened in 1892. Boxes of this type had large sliding windows three panes deep, and gable-ended slate roofs with spike finials at each end of the ridge. The main structure consisted of a wooden framework covered with horizontal boarding fixed on a dwarf brick wall. The name board was not under the windows but mounted - station name board style - beside the building, where it had a much better chance of being seen from passing trains. Despite being closed in 1967 this box, which contained a 'knee' frame of 6 levers, still stands at the time of writing, and serves as staff accommodation when the adjacent automatic half-barriers need to be placed on local control.
B.L. Jackson

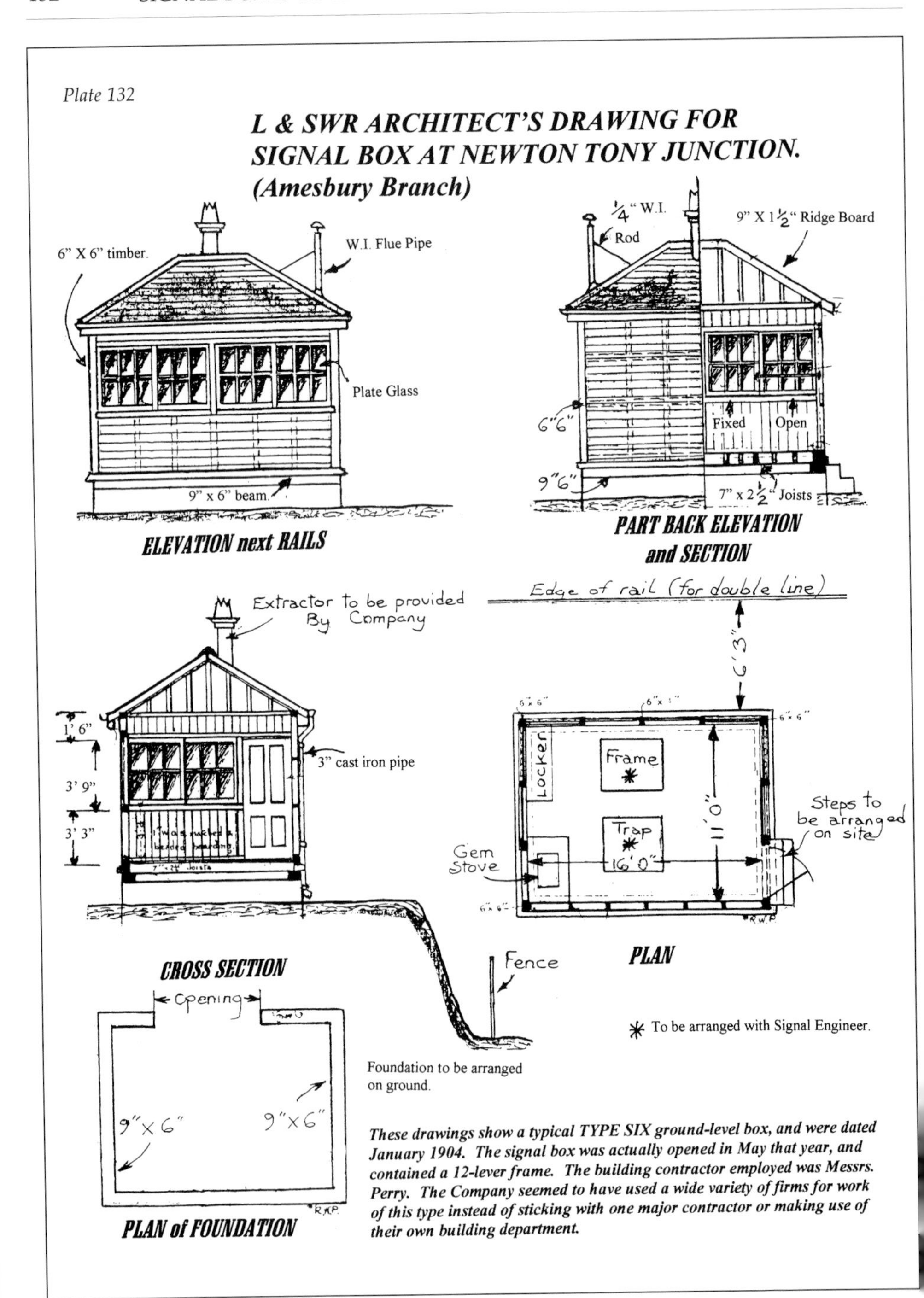

These drawings show a typical TYPE SIX ground-level box, and were dated January 1904. The signal box was actually opened in May that year, and contained a 12-lever frame. The building contractor employed was Messrs. Perry. The Company seemed to have used a wide variety of firms for work of this type instead of sticking with one major contractor or making use of their own building department.

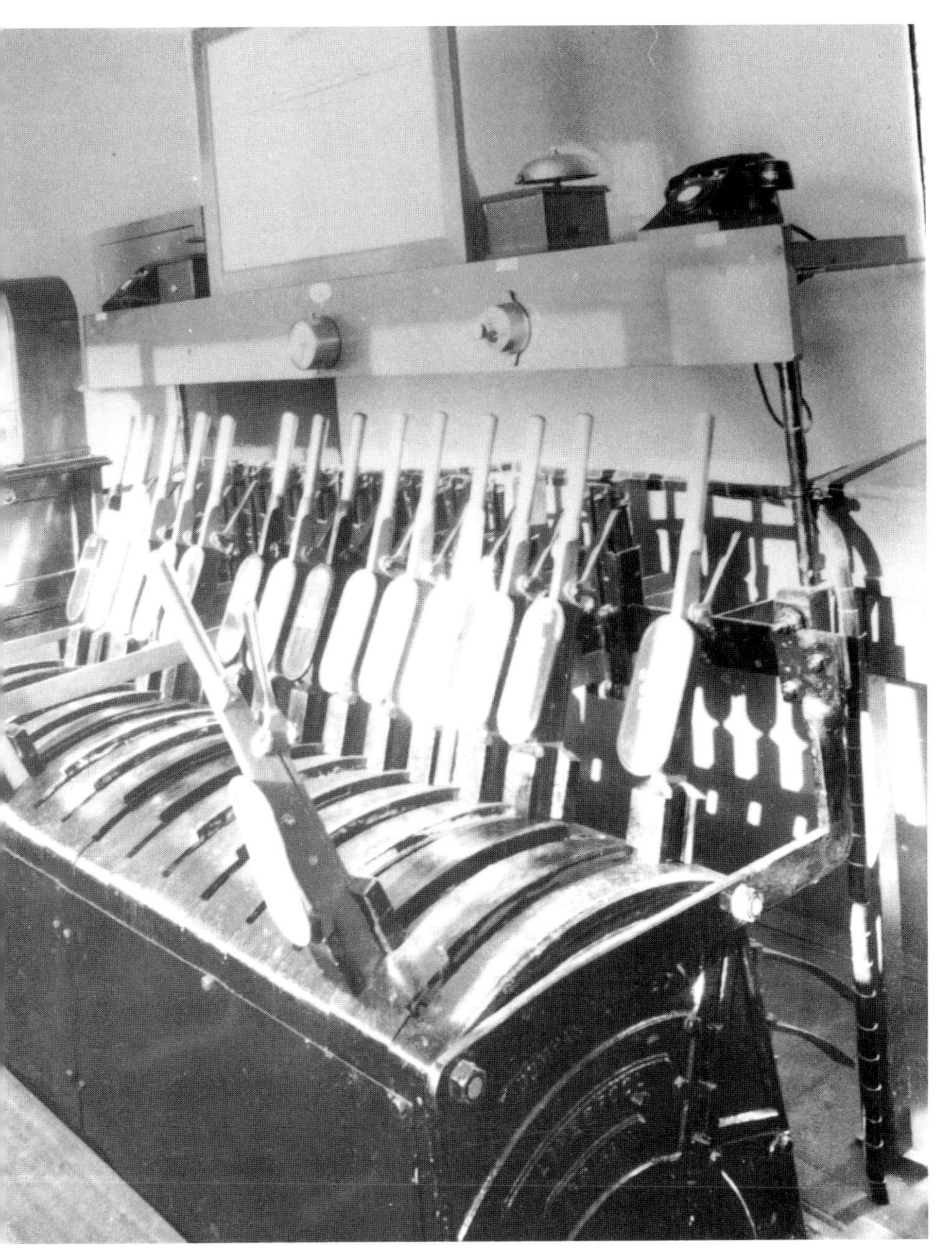

Plate 133: Ground level or 'knee' frame of the type used in boxes which had no room beneath the floor for conventional interlocking. Although this example at Lymington Pier was a BR installation dating from November 1956, it was almost certainly secondhand at that time and was exactly the same as those employed by the LSWR. This one was manufactured by the Railway Signal Company, but followed the Stevens' pattern. Several suppliers of these frames were active during the first half of the 20th century. Lymington Pier box was abolished on 4th March, 1968, having been reduced to a ground frame to control the adjacent level crossing the previous year. *Railtrack*

Plate 134: Type '6' box at Budleigh Salterton which had been opened in 1903 in connection with the extension of the branch to Exmouth. Boxes of this type had hipped slate roofs, often adorned with a standard LSWR vent, and sliding windows two panes deep. Otherwise the method of building was similar to that employed in the type '5s', except that the dwarf brick base wall sometimes came up higher from the ground. This box contained a 20-lever 'knee' frame, and lasted until closure of the line on 6th March, 1967.

A.E. West

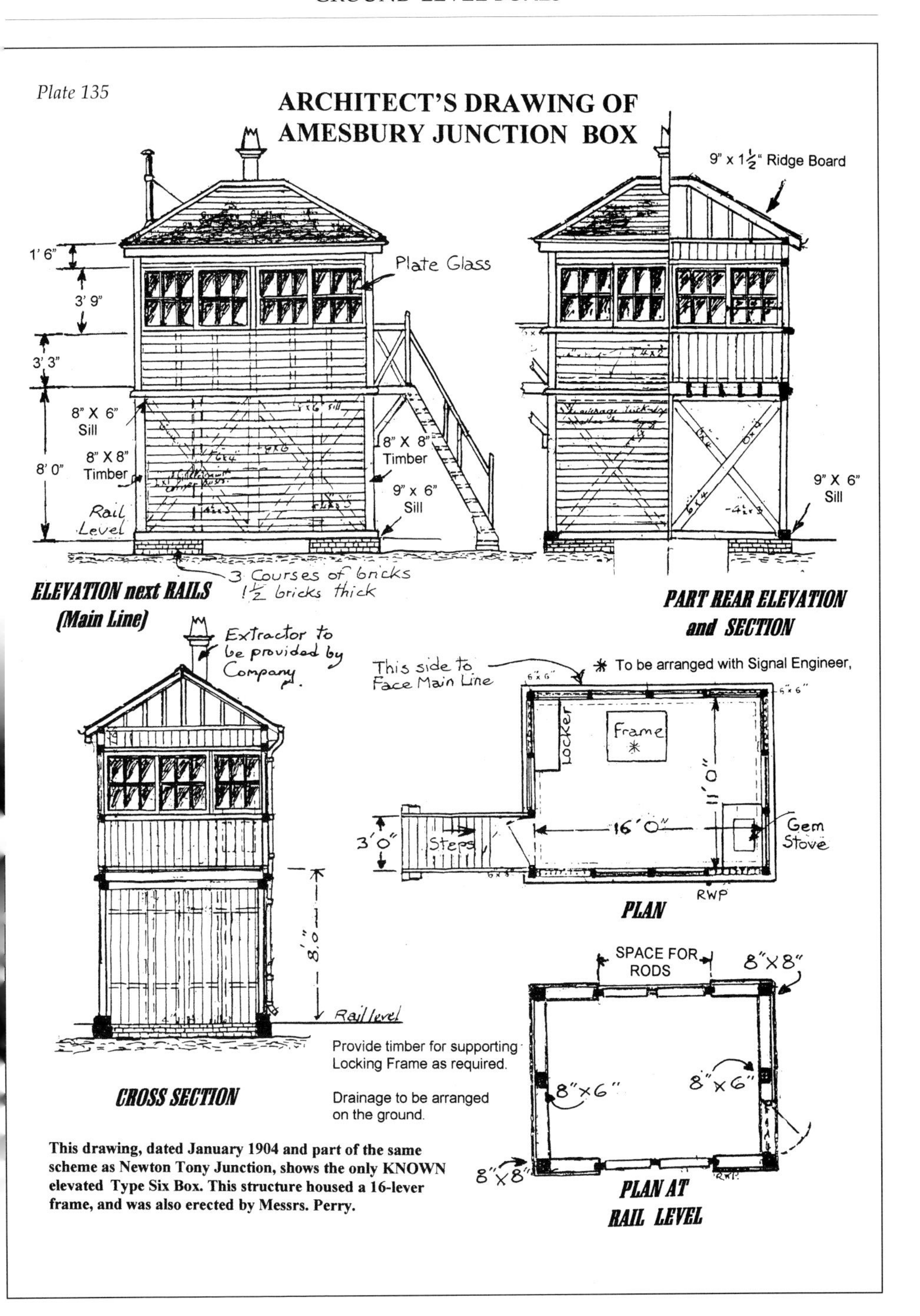

This drawing, dated January 1904 and part of the same scheme as Newton Tony Junction, shows the only KNOWN elevated Type Six Box. This structure housed a 16-lever frame, and was also erected by Messrs. Perry.

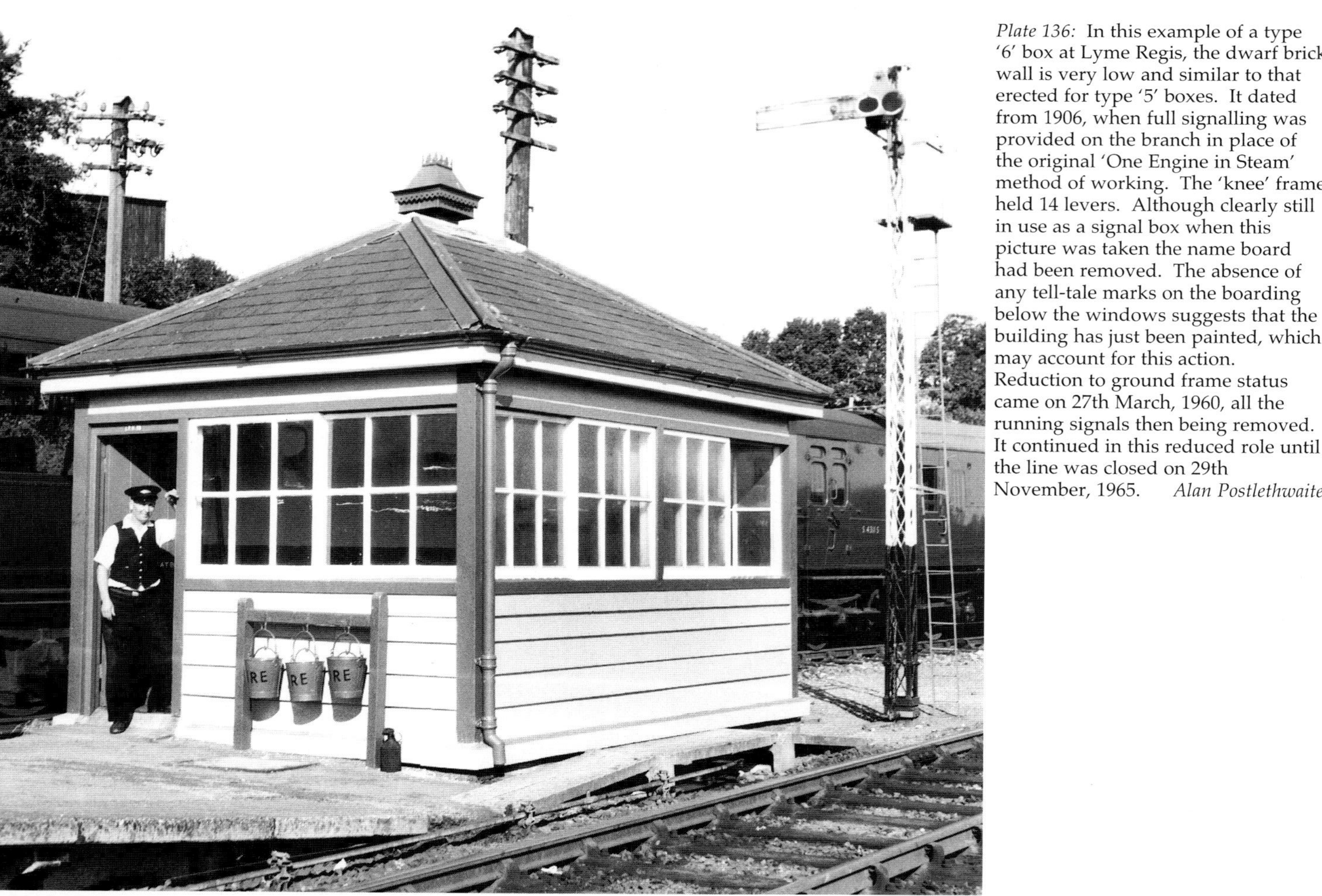

Plate 136: In this example of a type '6' box at Lyme Regis, the dwarf brick wall is very low and similar to that erected for type '5' boxes. It dated from 1906, when full signalling was provided on the branch in place of the original 'One Engine in Steam' method of working. The 'knee' frame held 14 levers. Although clearly still in use as a signal box when this picture was taken the name board had been removed. The absence of any tell-tale marks on the boarding below the windows suggests that the building has just been painted, which may account for this action. Reduction to ground frame status came on 27th March, 1960, all the running signals then being removed. It continued in this reduced role until the line was closed on 29th November, 1965. *Alan Postlethwaite*

Plate 137: Apart from the two standard designs, '5' and '6', ground-level boxes came in all shapes and sizes, some of them very interesting. Daggons Road was a unique structure with a curious curved roof covered with tarred canvas. It appears to have been opened in 1878, which makes it even stranger, as 'standard' designs were by then available. At first it contained 8 levers, and was a block post in connection with the Staff and Ticket system then in use on the line, but in August 1903 came the introduction of Tyer's electric tablet equipment and Daggons Road, which could not cross two trains, was reduced to a ground frame. In most cases where this happened much of the lever frame became spare, but here there were alterations to the layout and three levers were actually added! Although seldom used latterly, this unusual edifice remained officially in use until the West Moors-Alderbury Junction line closed on 4th May, 1964.

C.L. Caddy

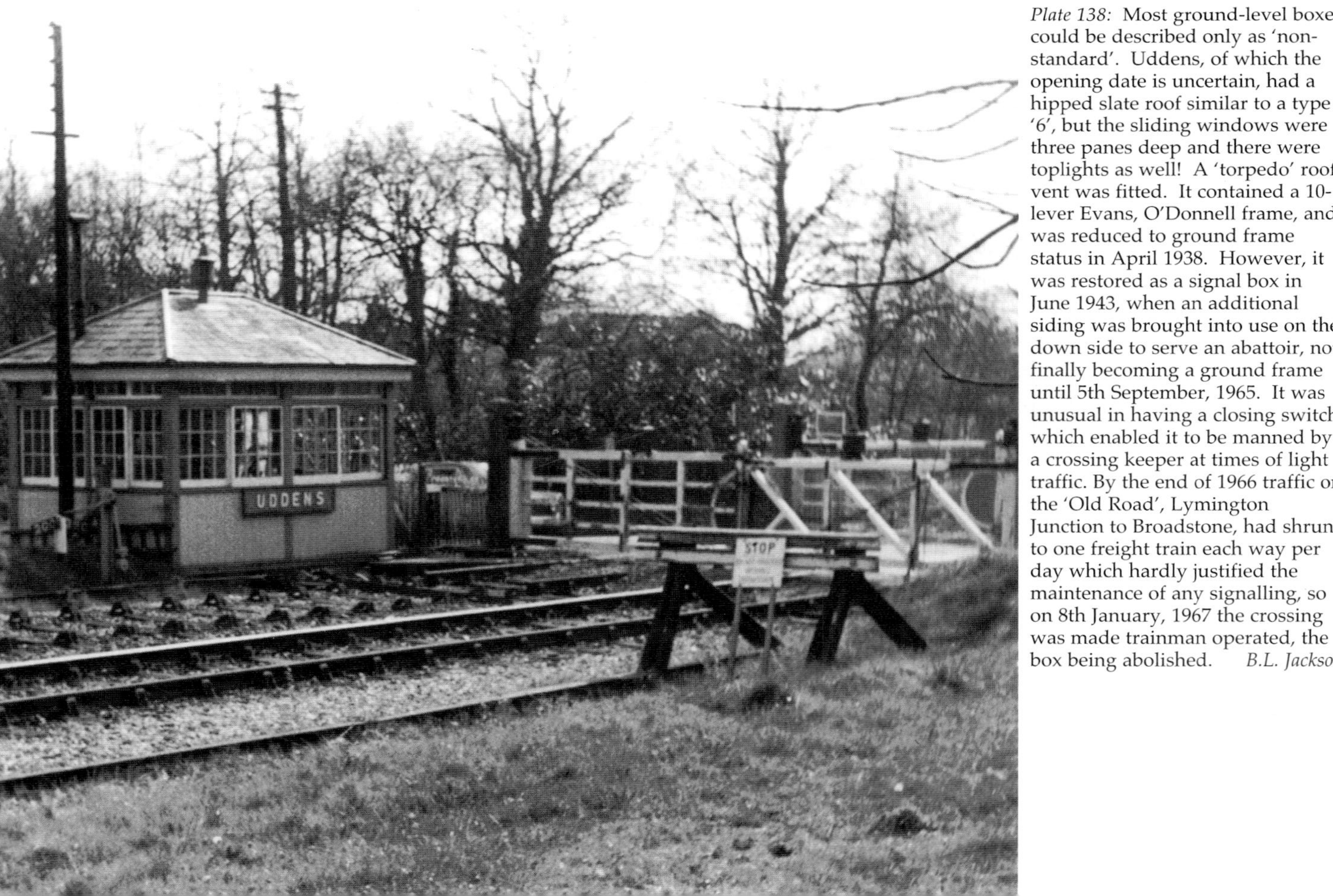

Plate 138: Most ground-level boxes could be described only as 'non-standard'. Uddens, of which the opening date is uncertain, had a hipped slate roof similar to a type '6', but the sliding windows were three panes deep and there were toplights as well! A 'torpedo' roof vent was fitted. It contained a 10-lever Evans, O'Donnell frame, and was reduced to ground frame status in April 1938. However, it was restored as a signal box in June 1943, when an additional siding was brought into use on the down side to serve an abattoir, not finally becoming a ground frame until 5th September, 1965. It was unusual in having a closing switch which enabled it to be manned by a crossing keeper at times of light traffic. By the end of 1966 traffic on the 'Old Road', Lymington Junction to Broadstone, had shrunk to one freight train each way per day which hardly justified the maintenance of any signalling, so on 8th January, 1967 the crossing was made trainman operated, the box being abolished. *B.L. Jackson*

Plate 139: No opening date is available for Crow Crossing, and the non-standard style makes it impossible to date. Probably it was pre-1893, as the opening of the Holes Bay Curve that year afforded a new through route to Weymouth via Bournemouth and traffic on the 'Old Road' declined thereafter, making it unlikely that any additional block posts would have been created later. This box, which contained 9 levers, was a timber structure on a dwarf brick wall with a hipped slate roof, stove-pipe chimney, and 'torpedo' vent. The windows were most unusual, being grouped at the ends almost type '4' style but with a central section of horizontal boarding and toplights which ran the entire length of the building. It was a block post until 17th June, 1936, but was worked as a ground frame from then until the line was taken out of use on 30th March, 1965. *C.L. Caddy*

Plate 140: Halterworth Crossing, near Romsey, was another totally non-standard ground-level crossing box of which the opening date is uncertain. Again the structure was mounted on a dwarf brick wall, but the space between it and the window sills was filled with plain wooden panels instead of the more usual horizontal boarding. Toplights were also much in evidence, although of a somewhat different pattern to those at either of the two previous examples. When the line was singled on 1st May, 1972 Halterworth ceased to be a block post, but the 7-lever box remained in use until the level crossing was converted to AHBs on 4th November, 1975.

R. Blencowe

Plate 141: Some ground-level boxes were distinctly shed-like. Waltham was a break-section box on the Southampton main line between Micheldever and Basingstoke which had been added in the 1890s in the face of ever-increasing traffic. As this picture shows, it was an all-timber building of very small proportions with a gable-ended slate roof, and probably changed very little throughout its life, except possibly for the front window frames which do not look original. It contained just 5 levers, although it did once control the connection to Steventon Manor Sidings as well as the running signals. It lasted until 13th November, 1966.

Oakwood Press Collection

Plate 142: Other signal boxes which would have done equally well as garden sheds could be found on the branch line from Bere Alston to Callington. This line had opened as a 3 ft 6 in. gauge mineral railway in 1872, and of course, not being a passenger line, had no signalling. However, in 1908 it was converted to standard guage and opened for passenger traffic, some cut-price signalling being installed for the occasion. Gunnislake, the largest of the three, was still pretty small! The garden shed-like structure and corrugated iron roof are suggestive of a temporary box, but it was there for 60 years, not closing until 5th May, 1968. It contained a 10-lever 'knee' frame.

J.H. Aston

Plate 143: A general view of Gunnislake station, looking towards Calstock, with the signal box on the left next to the buffer stops of the siding. Small and cheaply constructed as it was, it fitted in quite harmoniously with this tranquil branch line scene. *J.H. Aston*

Plate 144: Ground-level boxes were perhaps the most useful to purchasers of surplus equipment, and several of them found their way into farmyards and private gardens where they became tool sheds or small workshops. In 1906 the Lyme Regis branch was equipped with full signalling, type '6' boxes being opened both at the terminus and the intermediate station of Combpyne. This soon proved to be over-provision and Combpyne ceased to be a crossing place in August 1921, but it lingered on as a ground frame until 17th June, 1930 when an open 2-lever frame assumed control of the siding points. A local farmer was quick to see the potential of the building for some purpose of his own, buying it from the railway (doubtless at a bargain price) and transporting it to his yard nearby. This picture shows it 'down on the farm' in 1960, by which time it had become somewhat derelict.

Chapter Eight

Things that Happen

The closure of signal boxes in not a new phenomenon. It has been going on for practically a century, and there has been a variety of reasons for it. Most of the early casualties came about through track layout alterations such as quadrupling, the original boxes being much too small to cater for anything but minor expansion. When these alterations were made it often became possible to dispense with a few boxes, as the old Board of Trade limit for the mechanical working of points, a mere 100 yards, was gradually extended, at first to 200 yards, then 250, and finally to 350 yards. With the original limit all stations of any size had required two boxes, one at each end of the platform, but the later relaxations made it possible to control the whole complex from one carefully-positioned frame. Of course this reduced operating costs, saving not only the wages of signalmen but also considerable routine maintenance.

By the 1930s the point machine had achieved a high degree of reliability, and when used in conjunction with track circuits, allowed points to be operated at almost any distance from the controlling signal box. There was then even more scope for economies, and one only has to study the signalling history of such stations as Staines Central, Bournemouth Central, and Woking to appreciate how the use of electricity allowed the work of several mechanical boxes to be concentrated into one.

Track circuits also enabled the company to close many small section-splitting boxes, their functions being taken over by Intermediate Block Home signals controlled from the box in rear. These tiny boxes were usually in isolated locations and were difficult to staff in an age when the working man had no personal transport, so it made good sense to get rid of as many of them as possible. Many were closed, but a surprising number survived until the re-signalling of an area with colour-lights in modern times.

In recent years closures have come about through three main causes, and have tended to occur in waves. During the 1960s the closure of lines was an almost weekly occurrence, and a large number of boxes vanished with them. Often it was possible not only to abolish all the boxes on the closed line itself, but also to dispense with the one that had controlled its junction with the main line. One such closure could get rid of a dozen or more boxes in a single weekend. Another reason for mass box closures was the spread of multi-aspect signalling controlled from one panel, some of these schemes taking out 20 to 30 mechanical boxes and ground frames. In these cases not all the old boxes closed together, the work being staged over a number of weeks (or even months). The third and final reason has been a general reduction in traffic, or at least, the elimination of freight trains from whole areas of the railway system. Many lines have been left with nothing but a regular interval service of class '2' trains, making sidings and short block sections unnecessary and allowing the closure of most of the intermediate boxes. In most cases the simplification of the signalling has been carried out as a 'scheme', all the redundant boxes being abolished within a week or two of each other.

Plate 145: The type '5' box from Wyke Crossing (between Sherborne and Yeovil Junction) has been rather more lucky than Combpyne, although part of its story is similar. Opened around 1892 to control a very minor level crossing on the main line, it was abolished in December 1964 and soon found its way into the garden of an adjacent house where it served as a tool shed. By 1970 it had sunk into a ruinous condition, but managed to survive long enough to come to the notice of the local Signalling Manager who was heavily involved with the Gartell Light Railway, a narrow gauge line being constructed on part of the old Somerset & Dorset formation near Templecombe. Needing a box to control 'Pinesway Junction', the Gartell family made a successful bid for the building, which was subsequently moved to the Light Railway premises and reconstructed. Much of the original woodwork had decayed seriously and had to be renewed, and the box also had to be enlarged by inserting a central bay of windows, the new frame containing 30 levers as against the original one of just 7! The work was very skilfully done, and this box is likely to remain in use for many years to come. *R.L. Jackson*

But the issue of signal box closures in not a clear-cut one. Dates for stations are definite and their closures always call for comment in the local press, but signal boxes seldom made the news unless their end was spectacular in some way or caused major disruption to train services. Most boxes slid quietly into history, there one day and gone the next, and nobody took much notice. Sometimes 'closure' could be a protracted affair. A certain traffic would cease, and the signalman would be withdrawn. The 'Hours of Opening' booklet would proclaim 'Open as required', which in practice meant very seldom. Such a box could remain switched out of circuit for months (sometimes years) at a stretch, its signals poking skyward and its levers gradually becoming coated with a film of rust, but it was not actually 'closed'. In theory at least it was possible, provided a qualified signalman could be found, to open it to cover special traffic or engineering work. It could not be classified as 'Closed' until a team from the Signal Engineer's Department came along and dismantled the equipment, which sometimes happened several years after regular use of the box had been discontinued.

Over the years some strange things have happened to signal boxes. In some cases the long period of disuse prior to abolition encouraged the activities of vandals who damaged the building beyond economic repair, but others have met with an even more colourful end! There were other sources of damage, such as enemy action during World War II, and occasionally, the derailment of a train on an adjoining track. On the other hand some have been preserved, although not on their original sites, being removed piece by piece. The railway company occasionally re-sited boxes to save the expense of new structures, the buildings being jacked up and trundled a few yards in massive wooden cradles, but most of them were 'sold out of service' when no longer needed. The fate of these has been extremely varied. A few have been bought by preserved railways and re-erected for their original purpose, some ended up as outbuildings on farms or as potting sheds in the gardens of country houses, but a large number went as 'scrap'. The purchasers often had a bargain, a ready market existing for good-quality roof slates and well-seasoned woodwork, whilst the metal in the lever frame and its supports had considerable scrap value. The signalling instruments were never sold with the boxes, either being recovered by the Engineer for 'spares' or being sold at an inflated price to collectors of railwayana.

This short chapter sets out to illustrate not only some of the ways in which signal boxes met their ends, but also some of the more dramatic events in their lives. Fire does not seem to have played such a big part in the story of LSWR boxes as it did on many lines, notably the GWR, which is a little surprising in view of the largely timber construction of many of them together with the use of open fires and oil lamps! Where it has occurred it has usually been set deliberately by mindless vandals, but no photographs of a burned-out box have become available. At least one type '1' box - Broad Clyst - was set alight by the cinders from a passing train, but in that instance the Fire Brigade was swiftly summoned and the flames extinguished with only minor damage, much to the disgust of the area signal engineer who expressed a preference for letting it burn in the hope that he would then get a modern replacement!

Plate 146: Sometimes the Permanent Way Department found old signal boxes useful as mess rooms and tool stores, but they did not necessarily want the whole building. At Butts Junction (Alton) the 40-lever type '4' box was closed in February 1935. The upper storey was demolished, and the roof, complete with 'torpedo' vent, lowered onto the top of the locking room. It served the platelayers well for many years, but seems to have been disused by 1967 when this view was taken. It was later demolished.

B.L. Jackson

Plate 147: Whilst it was not uncommon for wooden signal boxes to be moved, those built partially of brick posed more of a problem, and usually it was easier to erect a completely new box. However, Wimbledon 'D' box was moved a distance of 12 feet on 27th February, 1928 to make room for an additional running line, these official photographs showing the stout wooden cradle in which the structure was encased to allow it to be moved on rollers. In its new position it lasted until 23rd May, 1982.

Railtrack

Plate 148: The signalman's ultimate nightmare was to have his box knocked from under him by a derailed train, and this was precisely what happened at Yeovil Junction West on the night of 4th July, 1914. An up freight had become divided approaching Sutton Bingham, the Yeovil signalman deciding to stop the front portion, probably on the through line, with the intention of diverting the rear onto the other line. However, it seems that things went wrong. The front part slowed down too quickly and was cannoned into by the loose-running back portion, the impact derailing the train just as the engine was passing the box. The wooden operating floor, a typical type '1' structure - was detached from its brick base and hurled halfway down the embankment, in which position it was captured by the local press photographer. Despite the widespread damage it remains possible to detect the extension added in 1909, and the fact that the box is still recognisable after such an impact says much for the strength and durability of these structures. This box was soon rebuilt with differences in detail yet retaining definite type '1' features (*see Plate 49*).

South Somerset District Council, Museum of South Somerset, Yeovil

Plare 149: Railways were obviously a legitimate target in times of war, but there were surprisingly few direct hits. Even this 1943 example, St Budeaux, was wrecked by blast damage, the bomb actually falling on the houses behind the box. Plymouth, with its large Royal Navy dockyard, had to suffer many air raids, but the LSWR lost only two boxes in the area as the result of enemy action, this one and Turnchapel. St Budeaux was quickly rebuilt with a lean-to roof, doubtless because of the shortage of materials and the urgency of getting the place functional again! *Railtrack*

Plate 150: London was the most dangerous place to be during the war, and the LSWR's habit of building signal boxes spanning the tracks on top of viaducts made the buildings rather vulnerable to attack from the air. To offer some protection the boxes were encased is blast-proof screens which made them reasonably safe from anything but a direct hit. These screens naturally made the buildings very dark, so with the return of peace they were removed to leave only the supporting framework. This view of Clapham Junction 'A' shows clearly what was done, and how the box remained for the rest of its life.

B.L. Jackson

Plate 151: When a signal box was finally closed it often found a buyer, elevated boxes usually being carefully dismantled by the purchaser for the good-quality materials the buildings contained. The price asked by the railway company was usually very modest, although a deadline for clearance of the site was generally stipulated. The type '3A' box at Moreton was closed on 16th February, 1972, and a contractor is seen here taking the place to pieces with rather more care than was usual in demolition work. No bulldozer or JCB here! The roof slates had already disappeared, doubtless being used again in repairing the roof of a period cottage, and the woodwork is being carefully salvaged. In those pre-Health & Safety days, nobody is wearing either high visibility clothing or hard hats, things that would be insisted upon today even if the work was being conducted under a total possession which closed the line to traffic.

Evan Jones

Bibliography and Acknowledgements

A work of this nature requires the consultation of many different publications as well as the help of individual experts. Many people have given their valuable time to answering my queries, and their efforts on my behalf are much appreciated. I will not mention the photographers here who have done so much to make this book worth looking at, as their names are given as credits against the appropriate pictures. Suffice it to say that their assistance has been invaluable.

Some useful information has come from both the Signalling Record Society and the South Western Circle, the latter especially, since their membership has a specialist interest in the old LSWR. Some of the architectural drawings of signal boxes reproduced in this volume have been supplied by that Society, whilst others have been 'dug out' from the Railtrack archives at Waterloo with the kind assistance of the manager of the Plan Arch.

Another valuable source of material, relating particularly to the older installations, has been the Public Record Office at Kew, where the 'MT6' files have been consulted on many occasions. Thanks go to Chris Hack for assisting me in this task during several visits. Thanks of a personal nature also go to Brian Jackson, fellow railway author from Dorset, who has spent much time and energy in tracking down obscure photographs.

Of the many publications consulted, the following have been especially useful:

An Illustrated History of Railways in Britain, G. Freeman Allen, (Marshall Cavendish, 1979)
The Signal Box, The Signalling Study Group (Oxford Publishing Co., 1986)
An Illustrated History of Signalling, Michael A. Vanns, (Ian Allan, 1997)
The Signalling Record, (Journal of the Signalling Record Society), various editions
The South Western Circular, (Journal of the South Western Circle), various editions

Finally, the author would like to express his appreciation of Ian Kennedy and all the staff at Oakwood Press for the initial suggestion of this book and their assistance and support throughout, and to Peter Whiting for undertaking the boring task of proof-reading.

Index

Note: Page numbers are shown in light type, plates numbers in bold type.

Further Study

Readers with a general interest in signalling, both in the UK and abroad, should consider joining the Signalling Record Society which was founded in 1969 for the detailed study of the subject. The membership secretary is Mr. B. Bridges, 38 Founcely Avenue, Dane End, Ware, Herts., SG12 ONQ.

Those seeking more information on specific locations are directed to a series of books entitled *Signal Box Diagrams of the Great Western & Southern Railways* which are available through the Oakwood Press. The series runs to 17 volumes at present, and covers she areas listed below. Each signal box within the specified geographical area is illustrated with a full signalling diagram showing all lever numbers, track circuits etc. together with opening and closing dates and notes on layout alterations and equipment. Ideal for the modeller who wants to get his signalling right, or for the transport historian. Each volume costs £6 except for those marked #, which are £5.50.

1. GWR Lines in Dorset
2. SR Lines in East Dorset#
3. Somerset & Dorset Joint Lines
4. GWR Westbury, Frome & Salisbury
5. SR Exeter to Templecombe (excl) & Branches#
6. GWR Exeter & Torbay#
7. SR Templecombe to Oakley & Branches#
8. GWR Taunton to Exeter & Branches#
9. SR Bournemouth to Southampton Central & Branches
10. GWR Bristol (excl) to Taunton & Branches#
11. SR in North Devon#
12. GWR in South Devon
13. SR Plymouth & North Cornwall
14. GWR Plymouth & East Cornwall
15. SR Southampton, Eastleigh, Winchester & Branches
16. GWR West Cornwall
17. SR in North Hampshire £7 (available shortly).

It is intended to gradually expand this series to cover the entire systems of both companies plus the LMS in the Bristol & Gloucester areas, but further publications will depend upon the success of the initial releases.

Note: Volumes 3, 7, 8 & 11 are currently out of print, but will be re-issued if demand is sufficient.